A Verilog® HDL Primer

Second Edition

Other books by the same author:

- *Verilog HDL Synthesis, A Practical Primer*, Star Galaxy Publishing, Allentown, PA 1998, ISBN 0-9650391-5-3.
- *A VHDL Primer, Third Edition*, Prentice Hall, Englewood Cliffs, NJ, 1999, ISBN 0-13-096575-8.
- *A VHDL Synthesis Primer, Second Edition*, Star Galaxy Publishing, Allentown, PA, 1998, ISBN 0-9650391-9-6.
- *A VHDL Synthesis Primer*, Star Galaxy Publishing, Allentown, PA, 1996, ISBN 0-9650391-0-2.
- *A Verilog HDL Primer, First Edition*, Star Galaxy Press, Allentown, PA, 1997, ISBN 0-9656277-4-8.
- *A VHDL Primer: Revised Edition*, Prentice Hall, Englewood Cliffs, NJ, 1995, ISBN 0-13-181447-8.
- *A Guide to VHDL Syntax*, Prentice Hall, Englewood Cliffs, NJ, 1995, ISBN 0-13-324351-6.
- *VHDL Features and Applications: Study Guide*, IEEE, 1995, Order No. HL5712.
- *A VHDL Primer*, Prentice Hall, Englewood Cliffs, NJ, 1992, ISBN 0-13-952987-X.
- **In Japanese**: *A VHDL Primer*, CQ Publishing, Japan, ISBN 4-7898-3286-4.
- **In German**: *Die VHDL-Syntax* (Translation of *A Guide to VHDL Syntax*), Prentice Hall Verlag GmbH, 1996, ISBN 3-8272-9528-9.

A
VERILOG HDL
PRIMER

SECOND EDITION

J. BHASKER

Bell Laboratories, Lucent Technologies

Star Galaxy Publishing
1058 Treeline Drive, Allentown, PA 18103

Published by:

Star Galaxy Publishing
1058 Treeline Drive, Allentown, PA 18103
Phone: 610-391-7296

WARNING - DISCLAIMER

The author and publisher have used their best efforts in preparing this book and the examples contained in it. They make no representation, however, that the examples are error-free or are suitable for every application to which a reader may attempt to apply them. The author and the publisher make no warranty of any kind, expressed or implied, with regard to these examples, documentation or theory contained in this book, all of which is provided "as is". The author and the publisher shall not be liable for any direct or indirect damages arising from any use, direct or indirect, of the examples provided in this book.

Verilog® is a registered trademark of Cadence Design Systems, Inc.
VeriBest® is a registered trademark of VeriBest, Inc.
Material in Appendix A is reprinted from IEEE Std 1364-1995 "IEEE Standard Hardware Description Language Based on the Verilog Hardware Description Language", Copyright © 1995 by the IEEE, Inc. The IEEE disclaims any responsibility or liability resulting from the placement and use in the described manner. Information is reprinted with the permission of the IEEE.

Printed in the United States of America

10 9 8 7 6 5 4 3

Library of Congress Catalog Card Number: 98-61678

ISBN 0-9650391-7-X

To my wife, Geetha

CONTENTS

CHAPTER 6

User-Defined Primitives   90

CHAPTER 7

Dataflow Modeling   98

CHAPTER 10

Other Topics   **161**

CHAPTER 11

Verification   207

CHAPTER 12

Modeling Examples   233

APPENDIX A

Syntax Reference   266

Bibliography   285

Index   287

PREFACE

Here is a neat and concise book that explains the basics of the Verilog hardware description language. The Verilog hardware description language, commonly and henceforth referred to as Verilog HDL, can be used to model digital designs at multiple levels of abstraction, ranging from the switch-level to the algorithmic-level. The language offers a powerful set of primitives, including logic gates and user-defined primitives, and a wide range of constructs that can be used to model not only the concurrent behavior of hardware but also its sequential nature and its structural composition. The language is also extensible via a programming language interface (PLI). Verilog HDL is a simple language to use but strong enough to model multiple levels of abstraction. The Verilog HDL language was standardized by the IEEE in 1995, called the IEEE Std 1364-1995; this book is based on this standard.

The purpose of this book is to introduce the Verilog hardware description language to the reader by explaining its basic and important constructs through examples. It is a primer. Each aspect of the language is described using clear, concise English so that it is easy to understand and not intimidating for a beginner. My hope is that this book can provide the very first step in learning Verilog HDL.

The book provides a thorough understanding of the basics of the Verilog language, both from the features point of view and its usage in modeling. A number of examples for each language construct is provided; in addition, examples are provided to illustrate how collectively constructs can be used to model hardware. The various modeling styles supported by Verilog HDL are described in detail. The book explains how stimulus and control can also be described using the same Verilog language, including response monitoring and verification. The syntax of many of the constructs are shown in an easy to read manner, sometimes although not complete. This is done purposely to help explain the construct. The complete syntax of constructs of the Verilog language is provided in an appendix for reference.

The book is not theoretical in nature and introduces the syntax and semantics of the language using common terms, rather than the technical jargon of the formal definition of the language. No attempt has been made to address the entire language, for example, features such as the programming language interface, switch-level modeling, and stochastic modeling are not described in this book. The book restricts itself to the most useful and common features of the language that are enough to model simple as well as complex devices.

This book is intended for hardware designers as well as others, including circuit and system designers and software tool developers, interested in learning to model hardware using Verilog HDL. The book can also be used as an introductory text in a first university course on computer-aided design, hardware modeling, or synthesis. It is well suited for working professionals as well as for undergraduate and graduate study. Designers can use this book as a way to get to know Verilog HDL and as a reference for work with Verilog HDL. Students and professors will find this book useful as a teaching tool for hardware design and for hardware description languages.

The book assumes a basic knowledge of digital hardware design as well as familiarity with a high-level programming language such as C.

Finally, I would like to comment that it is impractical to learn a language by reading alone. Typing out examples from this book and compiling and simulating them on a Verilog simulator is the best way to gain a complete and thorough understanding of the language. Once you have mastered this book, look at the IEEE Standard Language Reference Manual (LRM) for complete information on the Verilog HDL standard.

Book Organization

Chapter 1 provides a brief history of the language, describing its major capabilities.

Chapter 2 provides a quick overview of the language, by demonstrating the three main styles of describing a design: dataflow, behavioral, and structural style.

Chapter 3 describes the basic elements, that is, the nuts and bolts, of the language. It describes identifiers, comments, system tasks, compiler directives and data types, amongst others.

Chapter 4 is devoted solely to expressions. An expression can be used in many different places in a Verilog description, including delays. The chapter also describes the various kinds of operators and operands that can be used to form an expression.

Chapter 5 describes gate-level modeling, that is, modeling a design using built-in primitive gates. Gate delays are also explained. The concept of time and delay scaling is also introduced.

Verilog HDL provides the capability of creating user-defined primitives, that is, primitives in addition to the built-in primitives. This is the topic of Chapter 6. Combinational and sequential user-defined primitives are described with examples.

The dataflow modeling style is modeled using the continuous assignments in Verilog HDL. Chapter 7 describes this assignment and explains its execution semantics. Two kinds of delay, assignment delay and net delay, are described.

Chapter 8 describes the behavioral modeling style. It describes the two main procedural constructs: the initial statement and the always statement. The chapter also describes procedural assignments in detail. Sequential and parallel blocks are explained in detail with examples. High-level programming constructs such as conditional statement and loop statement are described in this chapter.

The structural style of modeling is elaborated in Chapter 9. The concept of hierarchy and matching of ports is examined in this chapter. Also included in this chapter is how modules connect with each other via port associations.

Advanced topics are presented in Chapter 10. Topics such as specify blocks, value change dump file, signal strengths are presented. This chapter also includes tasks and functions.

Chapter 11 and 12 are the most practical chapters since they talk about verification and modeling. Chapter 11 shows a number of test bench examples that show waveform generation and response monitoring. Chapter 12 shows a number of modeling examples that demonstrate the collective usage of Verilog language constructs.

Finally, Appendix A contains a complete syntax reference of the Verilog language. The grammar is described in Backus-Naur Form (BNF) and the constructs are all arranged alphabetically for easier search.

In all the Verilog HDL descriptions that appear in this book, reserved words, system tasks and system functions, and compiler directives are in **boldface**. In syntax descriptions, operators and punctuation marks that are part of the syntax are in boldface. Optional items in a grammar rule are indicated by using non-bold square brackets ([...]). Non-bold curly braces ({...}) identify items that are repeated zero or more times. Occasionally ellipsis (. . .) is used in Verilog HDL source to indicate code that is not relevant to that discussion. Certain words are written in `Courier` font to identify its Verilog meaning rather than its English meaning such as in `and` gate.

All examples in this book have been verified using the VeriBest® Verilog simulator, Version 14.0.

Acknowledgments

It is my pleasure to acknowledge the assistance of the following individuals who offered their valuable time and energy to review drafts of this manuscript despite their very busy schedule.

1. Brett Graves, Gabe Moretti and Doug Smith at VeriBest, Inc.
2. Stephanie Alter, Danny Johnson, Sanjana Nair, Carlos Roman, Mourad Takla, Jenjen Tiao and Sriram Tyagarajan at Bell Labs, Lucent Technologies, Inc.
3. Maqsoodul Mannan at National Semiconductor Corp.

This book owes a lot to their detailed comments and constructive criticism. I am gratefully indebted to them. Thank you very much!

I would like to thank Jean Dussault and Hao Nham for their continuous support and for providing a stimulating work atmosphere at Bell Labs.

Last, but not least, I would like to thank my wife, Geetha, and my two sons who gave me lots of emotional support, without which I would never have succeeded.

J. Bhasker
Allentown, PA
February 1997

Preface to Second Edition

This improved edition includes exercises for each and every chapter; this hopefully makes the book more useful in an university course. New sections on sharing tasks and functions, MOS switches, bidirectional switches, and named events, have been added. The page format and fonts have been redesigned to make the book more easier to read.

If you have any questions, comments or suggestions about the book, please feel free to contact me through my publisher.

J. Bhasker
January, 1999

❑

Chapter 1

INTRODUCTION

This chapter describes the history of the Verilog HDL language and it's major capabilities.

1.1 What is Verilog HDL?

Verilog HDL is a hardware description language that can be used to model a digital system at many levels of abstraction ranging from the algorithmic-level to the gate-level to the switch-level. The complexity of the digital system being modeled could vary from that of a simple gate to a complete electronic digital system, or anything in between. The digital system can be described hierarchically and timing can be explicitly modeled within the same description.

The Verilog HDL language includes capabilities to describe the behavioral nature of a design, the dataflow nature of a design, a design's structural composition, delays and a waveform generation mechanism including aspects of response monitoring and verification, all modeled using one single language. In addition, the language provides a programming language interface through which the internals of a design can be accessed during simulation including the control of a simulation run.

The language not only defines the syntax but also defines very clear simulation semantics for each language construct. Therefore, models written in this language can be verified using a Verilog simulator. The language inherits many of its operator symbols and constructs from the C programming language. Verilog HDL provides an extensive range of modeling capabilities, some of which are quite difficult to comprehend initially. However, a core subset of the language is quite easy to learn and use. This is sufficient to model most applications. The complete language, however, has sufficient capabilities to capture the descriptions from the most complex chips to a complete electronic system.

1.2   History

The Verilog HDL language was first developed by Gateway Design Automation[1] in 1983 as a hardware modeling language for their simulator product. At that time it was a proprietary language. Because of the popularity of their simulator product, Verilog HDL gained acceptance as a usable and practical language by a number of designers. In an effort to increase the popularity of the language, the language was placed in the public domain in 1990. Open Verilog International (OVI) was formed to promote Verilog. In 1992, OVI decided to pursue standardization of Verilog HDL as an IEEE standard. This effort was successful and the language became an IEEE standard in 1995. The complete standard is described in the Verilog Hardware Description Language Reference Manual. The standard is called IEEE Std 1364-1995.

1.3   Major Capabilities

Listed below are the major capabilities of the Verilog hardware description language:

---

1. Gateway Design Automation has since been acquired by Cadence Design Systems.

- Primitive logic gates, such as **and, or** and **nand**, are built-in into the language.

- Flexibility of creating a user-defined primitive (UDP). Such a primitive could either be a combinational logic primitive or a sequential logic primitive.

- Switch-level modeling primitive gates, such as **pmos** and **nmos**, are also built-in into the language.

- Explicit language constructs are provided for specifying pin-to-pin delays, path delays and timing checks of a design.

- A design can be modeled in three different styles or in a mixed style. These styles are: behavioral style - modeled using procedural constructs; dataflow style - modeled using continuous assignments; and structural style - modeled using gate and module instantiations.

- There are two data types in Verilog HDL; the net data type and the register data type. The net type represents a physical connection between structural elements while a register type represents an abstract data storage element.

- Hierarchical designs can be described, up to any level, using the module instantiation construct.

- A design can be of arbitrary size; the language does not impose a limit.

- Verilog HDL is non-proprietary and is an IEEE standard.

- It is human and machine readable. Thus it can be used as an exchange language between tools and designers.

- The capabilities of the Verilog HDL language can be further extended by using the programming language interface (PLI) mechanism. PLI is a collection of routines that allow foreign functions to access information within a Verilog module and allows for designer interaction with the simulator.

- A design can be described in a wide range of levels, ranging from switch-level, gate-level, register-transfer-level (RTL) to algorithmic-level, including process and queuing-level.

- A design can be modeled entirely at the switch-level using the built-in switch-level primitives.

- The same single language can be used to generate stimulus for the design and for specifying test constraints, such as specifying the values of inputs.

- Verilog HDL can be used to perform response monitoring of the design under test, that is, the values of a design under test can be monitored and displayed. These values can also be compared with expected values, and in case of a mismatch, a report message can be printed.

- At the behavioral-level, Verilog HDL can be used to describe a design not only at the RTL-level, but also at the architectural-level and its algorithmic-level behavior.

- At the structural-level, gate and module instantiations can be used.

- Figure 1-1 shows the mixed-level modeling capability of Verilog HDL, that is, in one design, each module may be modeled at a different level.

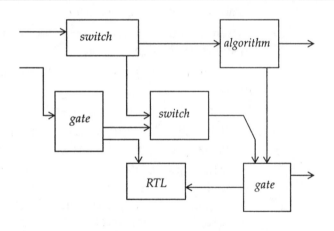

Figure 1-1   Mixed-level modeling.

- Verilog HDL also has built-in logic functions such as & (bitwise-and) and | (bitwise-or).

- High-level programming language constructs such as conditionals, case statements, and loops are available in the language.

- Notion of concurrency and time can be explicitly modeled.

- Powerful file read and write capabilities are provided.
- The language is non-deterministic under certain situations, that is, a model may produce different results on different simulators; for example, the ordering of events on an event queue is not defined by the standard.

1.4   Exercises

1. In which year was Verilog HDL first standardized by the IEEE?

2. What are the three basic description styles supported by Verilog HDL?

3. Can timing of a design be described using Verilog HDL?

4. What feature in the language can be used to describe parameterized designs?

5. Can a test bench be written using Verilog HDL?

6. Verilog HDL was first developed by which company?

7. What are the two main data types in Verilog HDL?

8. What does UDP stand for?

9. Name two switch-level modeling primitive gates.

10. Name two logic primitive gates.

❑

Chapter 2

A Tutorial

This chapter provides a quick tutorial of the language.

2.1   A Module

The basic unit of description in Verilog is the *module*. A module describes the functionality or structure of a design and also describes the ports through which it communicates externally with other modules. The structure of a design is described using switch-level primitives, gate-level primitives and user-defined primitives; dataflow behavior of a design is described using continuous assignments; sequential behavior is described using procedural constructs. A module can also be instantiated inside another module.

Here is the basic syntax of a module.

```
module module_name ( port_list ) ;
  Declarations:
    reg, wire, parameter,
    input, output, inout,
```

```
      function, task, . . .

    Statements:
      Initial statement
      Always statement
      Module instantiation
      Gate instantiation
      UDP instantiation
      Continuous assignment
endmodule
```

Declarations are used to define the various items, such as registers and parameters, used within the module. Statements are used to define the functionality or structure of the design. Declarations and statements can be interspersed within a module; however, a declaration must appear before its use. For clarity and readability it is best to put all declarations before any statements, and this convention is followed in all examples in this book.

Here is a simple example of a module that models the half-adder circuit shown in Figure 2-1.

```
module HalfAdder (A, B, Sum, Carry);
  input A, B;
  output Sum, Carry;

  assign #2 Sum = A ^ B;
  assign #5 Carry = A & B;
endmodule
```

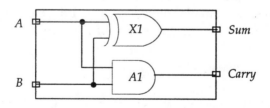

Figure 2-1   A half-adder circuit.

The name of the module is *HalfAdder*. It has four ports; two input ports *A* and *B*, and two output ports *Sum* and *Carry*. All ports are of size 1-bit since no range has been specified. Also, these four ports are of the net data type since no declaration has been specified.

The module contains two continuous assignment statements that describe the dataflow behavior of the half-adder. The statements are concurrent in the sense that their order of appearance within the module is not important. Execution of each statement occurs based on events occurring on nets A and B.

Within a module, a design can be described in the following styles:

    i.   Dataflow style

    ii. Behavioral style

    iii. Structural style

    iv. Any mix of above

The following sections describe these design styles with examples. But first, a little explanation about delays in Verilog HDL.

2.2   Delays

All delays in a Verilog HDL model are specified in terms of time units. Here is an example of a continuous assignment with a delay.

```
assign #2 Sum = A ^ B;
```

The #2 refers to 2 time units.

The association of a time unit with physical time is made using the `timescale compiler directive. Such a directive is specified before a module declaration. An example of such a directive is:

```
`timescale 1ns / 100ps
```

which says that one time unit is to be treated as 1ns and that the time precision is to be 100ps (the time precision says that all delays must be rounded to 0.1ns). If this compiler directive is present in the module containing the above continuous assignment, the #2 refers to 2ns.

If no such compiler directive is specified, a Verilog HDL simulator may default to a certain time unit; this default time unit is unspecified by the IEEE Verilog HDL standard.

2.3   Describing in Dataflow Style

The basic mechanism used to model a design in the dataflow style is the continuous assignment. In a continuous assignment, a value is assigned to a net. The syntax of a continuous assignment is:

assign [*delay*] *LHS_net = RHS_expression;*

Anytime the value of an operand used in the right-hand side expression changes, the right-hand side expression is evaluated, and the value is assigned to the left-hand side net after the specified delay. The delay specifies the time duration between a change of operand on the right-hand side and the assignment to the left-hand side. If no delay value is specified, the default is zero delay.

Here is an example of a 2-to-4 decoder circuit, shown in Figure 2-2, modeled using the dataflow style.

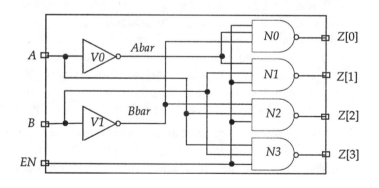

Figure 2-2   A 2-to-4 decoder circuit.

```
`timescale 1ns / 1ns
module Decoder2x4 (A, B, EN, Z);
  input A, B, EN;
  output [0:3] Z;
  wire Abar, Bbar;

  assign #1 Abar = ~A;                    // Stmt 1.
  assign #1 Bbar = ~B;                    // Stmt 2.
  assign #2 Z[0] = ~ (Abar & Bbar & EN);  // Stmt 3.
  assign #2 Z[1] = ~ (Abar & B & EN);     // Stmt 4.
  assign #2 Z[2] = ~ (A & Bbar & EN);     // Stmt 5.
  assign #2 Z[3] = ~ (A & B & EN);        // Stmt 6.
endmodule
```

The first statement, the one that begins with a backquote, is an example of a compiler directive. The compiler directive `timescale sets the time unit in the module for all delays to be 1ns and the time precision to be 1ns. For example, the delay values #1 and #2 in the continuous assignments correspond to delay values of 1ns and 2ns respectively.

The module *Decoder2x4* has three input ports and one 4-bit output port. A net declaration declares the two wires *Abar* and *Bbar* (a wire is one of the net types). In addition, the module contains six continuous assignment statements.

See the waveforms in Figure 2-3. When *EN* changes at 5ns, statements 3, 4, 5, and 6 are executed; this is because *EN* is an operand on the right-hand side of each of these continuous assignments. $Z[0]$ gets assigned to its new value, which is 0, at time 7ns. When *A* changes at 15ns, statements 1, 5 and 6 execute. Execution of statements 5 and 6 do not affect the value of $Z[0]$ and $Z[1]$. Execution of statement 5 causes $Z[2]$ to change to 0 at 17ns. Execution of statement 1 causes *Abar* to get its new value at time 16ns. Since *Abar* changes, this in turn causes $Z[0]$ to change value to 1 at time 18ns.

Notice that the continuous assignments model dataflow behavior of the circuit; the structure is implicit, not explicit. In addition, continuous assignments execute concurrently, that is, they are order-independent.

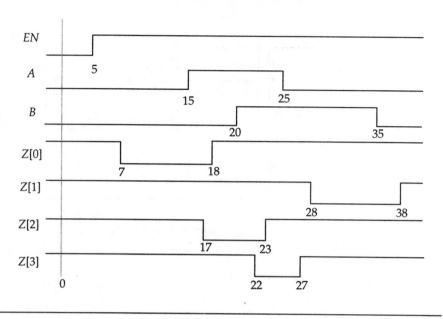

Figure 2-3 Example of continuous assignments.

2.4   Describing in Behavioral Style

The behavior of a design is described using procedural constructs. These are:

i.   Initial statement: This statement executes only once.

ii.   Always statement: This statement always executes in a loop, that is, the statement is executed repeatedly.

Only a register data type can be assigned a value in either of these statements. Such a data type retains its value until a new value is assigned. All initial statements and always statements begin execution at time 0 concurrently.

Here is an example of an always statement used to model the behavior of a 1-bit full-adder circuit shown in Figure 2-4.

```
module FA_Seq (A, B, Cin, Sum, Cout);
  input A, B, Cin;
  output Sum, Cout;
```

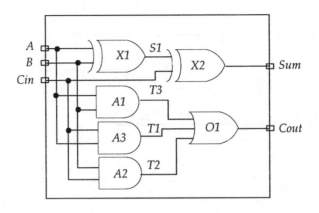

Figure 2-4   A 1-bit full-adder.

```
reg Sum, Cout;
reg T1, T2, T3;

always
  @ (A or B or Cin) begin
    Sum = (A ^ B) ^ Cin;
    T1 = A & Cin;
    T2 = B & Cin;
    T3 = A & B;
    Cout = (T1 | T2) | T3;
  end
endmodule
```

The module *FA_Seq* has three inputs and two outputs. *Sum*, *Cout*, *T1*, *T2* and *T3* are declared to be of type **reg** (**reg** is one of the register data types) because these are assigned values within the always statement. The always statement has a sequential block (**begin-end** pair) associated with an event control (the expression following the @ character). This means that whenever an event occurs on *A*, *B* or *Cin*, the sequential block is executed. Statements within a sequential block execute sequentially and the execution suspends after the last statement in the sequential block has executed. After the sequential block completes execution, the always statement again waits for an event to occur on *A*, *B*, or *Cin*.

The statements that appear within the sequential block are examples of blocking procedural assignments. A blocking procedural assignment completes execution before the next statement executes. A procedural assignment may optionally have a delay.

Delays can be specified in two different forms:

i.   Inter-statement delay: This is the delay by which a statement's execution is delayed.

ii. Intra-statement delay: This is the delay between computing the value of the right-hand side expression and its assignment to the left-hand side.

Here is an example of an inter-statement delay.

```
Sum = (A ^ B) ^ Cin;
#4 T1 = A & Cin;
```

The delay in the second statement specifies that the execution of the assignment is to be delayed by 4 time units. That is, after the first statement executes, wait for 4 time units, and then execute the second assignment. Here is an example of intra-statement delay.

```
Sum = #3 (A ^ B) ^ Cin;
```

The delay in this assignment means that the value of the right-hand side expression is to be computed first, wait for 3 time units, and then assign the value to *Sum*.

If no delays are specified in a procedural assignment, zero delay is the default, that is, assignment occurs instantaneously. More on this and other forms of statements that can be specified in an always statement are discussed in Chapter 8.

Here is an example of an initial statement.

```
`timescale 1ns / 1ns
module Test (Pop, Pid);
  output Pop, Pid;
  reg Pop, Pid;

  initial
  begin
    Pop = 0;          // Stmt 1
    Pid = 0;          // Stmt 2
```

```
        Pop = #5 1;      // Stmt 3
        Pid = #3 1;      // Stmt 4
        Pop = #6 0;      // Stmt 5
        Pid = #2 0;      // Stmt 6
    end
endmodule
```

This module generates the waveforms shown in Figure 2-5. The initial statement contains a sequential block which starts execution at time 0ns and after it completes executing all statements within the sequential block, the initial statement suspends forever. This sequential block contains examples of blocking procedural assignments with intra-statement delays specified. Statements 1 and 2 execute at time 0ns. The execution of the third statement, also at time 0, causes *Pop* to get assigned a value at time 5ns. Statement 4 executes at 5ns, and *Pid* gets assigned the value at 8ns. Similarly, *Pop* gets the value 0 at 14ns and *Pid* gets the value 0 at 16ns. After statement 6 executes, the initial statement suspends forever. Chapter 8 describes initial statement in more detail.

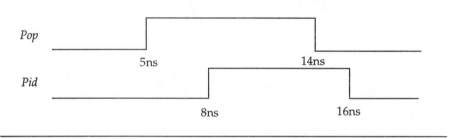

Figure 2-5   Output of module *Test*.

2.5   Describing in Structural Style

Structure can be described in Verilog HDL using:

i.   Built-in gate primitives (at the gate-level)

ii. Switch-level primitives (at the transistor-level)

iii. User-defined primitives (at the gate-level)

iv. Module instances (to create hierarchy)

Interconnections are specified by using nets. Here is an example of a full-adder circuit described in a structural fashion using built-in gate primitives and based on the logic diagram shown in Figure 2-4.

```
module FA_Str (A, B, Cin, Sum, Cout);
  input A, B, Cin;
  output Sum, Cout;
  wire S1, T1, T2, T3;

  xor
    X1 (S1, A, B),
    X2 (Sum, S1, Cin);

  and
    A1 (T3, A, B),
    A2 (T2, B, Cin),
    A3 (T1, A, Cin);

  or
    O1 (Cout, T1, T2, T3);
endmodule
```

In this example, the module contains gate instantiations, that is, instances of built-in gates **xor**, **and**, and **or**. The gate instances are interconnected by nets *S1*, *T1*, *T2*, and *T3*. The gate instantiations can appear in any order since no sequentiality is implied; pure structure is being shown; **xor**, **and** and **or** are built-in gate primitives; *X1*, *X2*, *A1*, etc. are the instance names. The list of signals following each gate are its interconnections; the first one is the output of the gate and the rest are its inputs. For example, *S1* is connected to the output of the xor gate instance *X1* while *A* and *B* are connected to its inputs.

A 4-bit full-adder can be described by instantiating four 1-bit full-adder modules, the logic diagram of which is shown in Figure 2-6. The model of this 4-bit full-adder is shown next.

```
module FourBitFA (FA, FB, FCin, FSum, FCout);
  parameter SIZE = 4;
  input [SIZE:1] FA, FB;
  output [SIZE:1] FSum;
  input FCin;
  input FCout;
  wire [1:SIZE-1] FTemp;
```

15

```
FA_Str
  FA1 (.A(FA[1]), .B(FB[1]), .Cin(FCin),
       .Sum(FSum[1]), .Cout(FTemp[1])),
  FA2 (.A(FA[2]), .B(FB[2]), .Cin(FTemp[1]),
       .Sum(FSum[2]), .Cout(FTemp[2])),
  FA3 (FA[3], FB[3], FTemp[2], FSum[3], FTemp[3]),
  FA4 (FA[4], FB[4], FTemp[3],FSum[4], FCout);
endmodule
```

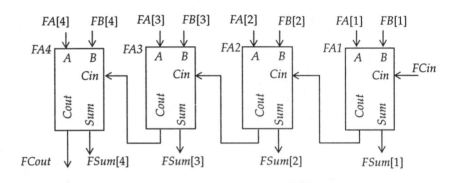

Figure 2-6   A 4-bit full-adder.

In this example, module instantiations are used to model a 4-bit full-adder. In a module instantiation, the ports can be associated by name or by position. The first two instantiations *FA1* and *FA2* use named associations, that is, the name of the port and the net to which it is connected to are explicitly described (each is of the form ". *port_name* (*net_name*)"). The last two instantiations, instances *FA3* and *FA4*, associate ports with nets using positional association. The order of the associations is important here, for example, in instance *FA4*, the first one *FA*[4] is connected to port *A* of *FA_Str*, the second one *FB*[4] is connected to port *B* of *FA_Str*, and so on.

2.6   Describing in Mixed-design Style

Within a module, structural and behavioral constructs can be mixed freely, that is, a module can contain a mixture of gate instantiations, module instantiations, continuous assignments, and always and initial statements, amongst others. Values from always statements and initial statements (remember only a register data type can be assigned a value within these statements) can drive gates or switches, while values from gates or continuous assignments (can only drive nets) can in turn be used to trigger always statements and initial statements.

Here is an example of a 1-bit full-adder in a mixed-design style.

```
module FA_Mix (A, B, Cin, Sum, Cout);
  input A, B, Cin;
  output Sum, Cout;
  reg Cout;
  reg T1, T2, T3;
  wire S1;

  xor X1 (S1, A, B);        // Gate instantiation.

  always
    @ (A or B or Cin) begin  // Always statement.
      T1 = A & Cin;
      T2 = B & Cin;
      T3 = A & B;
      Cout = (T1 | T2) | T3;
    end

  assign Sum = S1 ^ Cin;     // Continuous assignment.
endmodule
```

Execution of the gate instantiation occurs whenever an event occurs on *A* or *B*. The always statement executes whenever there is an event on *A*, *B* or *Cin*, and the continuous assignment executes whenever there is an event on *S1* or *Cin*.

2.7   Simulating a Design

Verilog HDL provides capabilities not only to describe a design but also to model stimulus, control, storing responses and verification, all using the same language. Stimulus and control can be generated using initial statements. Responses from the design under test can be saved as "save on change" or as strobed data. Finally, verification can be performed by automatically comparing with expected responses by writing appropriate statements in an initial statement.

Here is an example of a test module *Top* that tests the module *FA_Seq* described earlier in Section 2.3.

```
`timescale 1ns/1ns
module Top;          // A module may have an empty port list.
  reg PA, PB, PCi;
  wire PCo, PSum;

// Instantiate module under test:
FA_Seq F1 (PA, PB, PCi, PSum, PCo); // Positional.

initial
  begin: ONLY_ONCE
    reg [3:0] Pal;
      // Need 4 bits so that Pal can have the value 8.

    for (Pal = 0; Pal < 8; Pal = Pal + 1)
      begin
        {PA, PB, PCi} = Pal;
        #5 $display ("PA, PB, PCi=%b%b%b", PA, PB, PCi,
                     " ::: PCo, PSum=%b%b", PCo, PSum);
      end
  end
endmodule
```

The signals in the module instantiation are linked to the ports of the module under test using positional association, that is, *PA* is connected to port *A* of module *FA_Seq*, *PB* is connected to port *B* of module *FA_Seq*, and so on. Notice that a for-loop statement has been used in the initial statement to generate a waveform on *PA*, *PB* and *PCi*. The target of the first assignment statement within the for-loop represents a concatenated target. The appropriate bits on the right-hand side are assigned to the left-hand side argument from right to left. The initial statement also contains an example of a predefined system task. The $**display** system task prints the specified argument values in the specified format to the output.

The delay control in the $**display** system task call specifies that the $**display** task is to be executed after 5 time units. This 5 time units basically represents the settling time for the logic, that is, the delay time between the application of a vector and observing the module-under-test's response.

There is yet another nuance to this model. *Pal* is declared locally within the initial statement. To do this, the sequential block (**begin-end**) in the initial statement has to be labeled. *ONLY_ONCE* is the block label in this case. The block label is not necessary if there are no variables declared locally within the block. Figure 2-7 shows the waveforms produced. Here is the output produced by the test module.

```
PA, PB, PCi =000 ::: PCo, PSum =00
PA, PB, PCi =001 ::: PCo, PSum =01
PA, PB, PCi =010 ::: PCo, PSum =01
PA, PB, PCi =011 ::: PCo, PSum =10
PA, PB, PCi =100 ::: PCo, PSum =01
PA, PB, PCi =101 ::: PCo, PSum =10
PA, PB, PCi =110 ::: PCo, PSum =10
PA, PB, PCi =111 ::: PCo, PSum =11
```

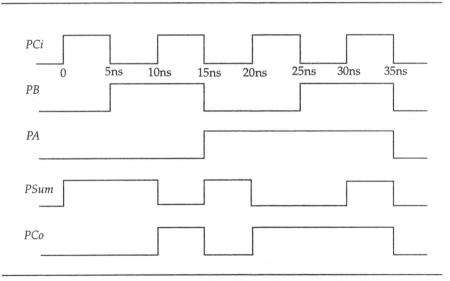

Figure 2-7 Waveforms produced by executing test bench *Top*.

Here is another example of a test module that exercises the cross-coupled nand gate module *RS_FF* shown in Figure 2-8.

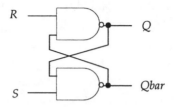

Figure 2-8   Cross-coupled nand gates.

```
`timescale 10ns/1ns
module RS_FF (Q, Qbar, R, S);
  output Q, Qbar;
  input R, S;

  nand #1 (Q, R, Qbar);
  nand #1 (Qbar, S, Q);
    // Instance names are optional in gate instantiations.
endmodule

module Test;
  reg TS, TR;
  wire TQ, TQb;

  // Instantiate module under test:
  RS_FF NSTA (.Q(TQ), .S(TS), .R(TR), .Qbar(TQb));
    // Using named association.

  // Apply stimulus:
  initial
    begin
      TR = 0;
      TS = 0;
      #5 TS = 1;
      #5 TS = 0;
      TR = 1;
      #5 TS = 1;
      TR = 0;
      #5 TS = 0;
      #5 TR = 1;
    end
```

```
// Display output:
initial
  $monitor ("At time %t,", $time,
    " TR=%b, TS=%b, TQ=%b, TQb=%b", TR, TS, TQ, TQb);
endmodule
```

Module *RS_FF* describes the structure of the design. Gate delays are used in gate instantiations; for example, the gate delay for the first instantiation is 1 time unit. This gate delay implies that if *R* or *Qbar* changes at say time *T*, then *Q* gets the computed value at time *T*+1.

The module *Test* is the test module. The design under test *RS_FF* is instantiated and its ports are connected using named association. There are two initial statements in this module. The first initial statement simply generates the waveform on *TS* and *TR*. This initial statement contains blocking procedural assignments with inter-statement delays.

The second initial statement is used to call the system task **$monitor**. This task when called causes the specified string to be printed whenever a change occurs in the specified variables in the argument list. Figure 2-9 shows the waveforms produced. Here is the output produced by the test module. Notice the effect produced by the `**timescale** directive on the delays.

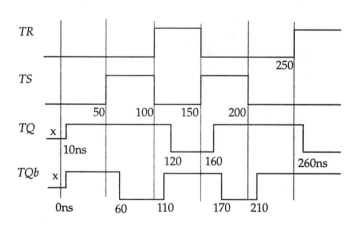

Figure 2-9 Waveforms produced by module *Test*.

```
At time        0, TR=0, TS=0, TQ=x, TQb=x
At time        10, TR=0, TS=0, TQ=1, TQb=1
At time        50, TR=0, TS=1, TQ=1, TQb=1
```

At time	60, TR=0, TS=1, TQ=1, TQb=0
At time	100, TR=1, TS=0, TQ=1, TQb=0
At time	110, TR=1, TS=0, TQ=1, TQb=1
At time	120, TR=1, TS=0, TQ=0, TQb=1
At time	150, TR=0, TS=1, TQ=0, TQb=1
At time	160, TR=0, TS=1, TQ=1, TQb=1
At time	170, TR=0, TS=1, TQ=1, TQb=0
At time	200, TR=0, TS=0, TQ=1, TQb=0
At time	210, TR=0, TS=0, TQ=1, TQb=1
At time	250, TR=1, TS=0, TQ=1, TQb=1
At time	260, TR=1, TS=0, TQ=0, TQb=1

The following chapters elaborate on these topics and more in greater detail.

2.8   Exercises

1. What statement is used to describe a design in the dataflow style?

2. What is the purpose of the `timescale compiler directive? Give an example.

3. What are the two kinds of delays that can be specified in a procedural assignment statement? Elaborate using an example.

4. Describe the 1-bit full-adder shown in Figure 2-4 using the dataflow style.

5. What is the key difference between an initial statement and an always statement?

6. Generate the following waveform on a variable *BullsEye* using an initial statement.

Figure 2-10 A waveform on variable *BullsEye*.

7. Write a model, in structural style, for the 2-to-4 decoder shown in Figure 2-2.

8. Write a test bench to test the module *Decoder2x4* described in Section 2.3.

9. Name two kinds of assignment statements that you can have in a Verilog HDL model.

10. When is a label required to be specified in a sequential block?

11. Using the dataflow description style, write a Verilog HDL model for the following exclusive-or logic. Use the specified delays.

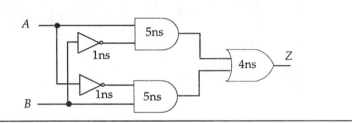

Figure 2-11 Exclusive-or logic.

12. What is wrong with the following continuous assignment?

```
assign Reset = #2 ^ WriteBus;
```

Chapter 3

LANGUAGE ELEMENTS

This chapter describes the basic elements of Verilog HDL. It introduces identifiers, comments, numbers, compiler directives, system tasks and system functions. In addition, it introduces the two data types in the language.

3.1   Identifiers

An *identifier* in Verilog HDL is any sequence of letters, digits, the $ character, and the _ (underscore) character, with the restriction that the first character must be a letter or an underscore. In addition, *identifiers are case-sensitive*. Here are some examples of identifiers.

```
Count
COUNT           // Distinct from Count.
_R2_D2
R56_68
FIVE$
```

An *escaped identifie*r provides a way of including any of the printable ASCII characters in an identifier. An escaped identifier starts with a \ (backslash) character and ends with a white space (a *white space* is a space, tab or a newline). Here are some examples of escaped identifiers.

```
\7400
\.*.$
\{******}
\~Q
\OutGate          is same as    OutGate
```

The last example explains the fact that, in an escaped identifier, the backslash and the terminating space are not part of the identifier. Thus, identifier *OutGate* is identical to identifier *OutGate*.

Verilog HDL defines a list of reserved identifiers, called *keywords*, that can only be used in certain contexts. Appendix A lists all the reserved words in the language. Note that only the lower case keywords are reserved words. For example, identifier **always** (which is a keyword) is distinct from the identifier *ALWAYS* (which is not a keyword).

In addition, an escaped keyword is not treated the same as the keyword. Thus, identifier \initial is distinct from the identifier **initial** (which is a keyword). Note that this convention is different from those of escaped identifiers.

3.2   Comments

There are two forms of comments in Verilog HDL.

```
/* First form: Can
   extend across
   many
   lines */


// Second form: Ends at the end of this line.
```

3.3   Format

Verilog HDL is case-sensitive. That is, identifiers differing only in their case are distinct. In addition, Verilog HDL is free-format, that is, constructs may be written across multiple lines, or on one line. White space (newline, tab, and space characters) have no special significance. Here is an example that illustrates this.

initial begin *Top* = 3'b001; #2 *Top* = 3'b011; **end**

is same as:

```
initial
  begin
    Top = 3'b001;
    #2 Top = 3'b011;
  end
```

3.4   System Tasks and Functions

An identifier beginning with a $ character is interpreted as a system task or as a system function. A task provides a mechanism to encapsulate a behavior that can be invoked from different parts of a design. A task can return zero or more values. A function is like a task except that it can return only one value. In addition, a function executes in zero time, that is, no delays are allowed, while a task can have delays.

```
$display ("Hi, you have reached LT today");
/* The $display system task displays the specified message
   to output with a newline character. */

$time
// This system function returns the current simulation time.
```

Tasks and functions are described in Chapter 10.

3.5   Compiler Directives

Certain identifiers that start with the ` (backquote) character are compiler directives. A compiler directive, when compiled, remains in effect through the entire compilation process (which could span multiple files) until a different compiler directive specifies otherwise. Here is a complete list of standard compiler directives.

- `define, `undef
- `ifdef, `else, `endif
- `default_nettype
- `include
- `resetall
- `timescale
- `unconnected_drive, `nounconnected_drive
- `celldefine, `endcelldefine

3.5.1   `define and `undef

The `define directive is used for text substitution and is very much like the #define in the C programming language. Here is an example of this directive.

```
`define MAX_BUS_SIZE 32
. . .
reg [ `MAX_BUS_SIZE - 1 : 0 ] AddReg;
```

Once the `define directive is compiled, the definition stays in effect through the entire compilation. For example the usage of *MAX_BUS_SIZE* could be across many different files with the `define directive in another file.

The `undef directive removes the definition of a previously defined text macro. Here is an example.

```
`define WORD 16    // Creates a macro for text substitution.
. . .
wire [ `WORD : 1 ] Bus;
. . .
`undef WORD
```

```
// The definition of WORD is no longer available
// after this `undef directive.
```

3.5.2   `ifdef, `else and `endif

These compiler directives are used for conditional compilation. Here is an example.

```
`ifdef WINDOWS
  parameter WORD_SIZE = 16;
`else
  parameter WORD_SIZE = 32;
`endif
```

During compilation, if the text macro name *WINDOWS* is defined, the first parameter declaration is selected, otherwise the second parameter declaration is selected.

The `else directive is optional with the `ifdef directive.

3.5.3   `default_nettype

This directive is used to specify the net type for implicit net declarations, that is, for nets that are not declared.

```
`default_nettype wand
```

This example specifies the default net type to be a wand net. Therefore, if a net is not declared in any module following this directive, the net is assumed to be a wand net.

3.5.4   `include

The `include compiler directive can be used to include the contents of any file in-line. The file can be specified either with a relative path name or with a full path name.

```
`include "../../primitives.v"
```

Upon compilation, this line is replaced with the contents of the file "../../primitives.v".

3.5.5 `resetall

This compiler directive resets all compiler directives to their default value.

```
`resetall
```

For example, this directive causes the default net type to be wire.

3.5.6 `timescale

In a Verilog HDL model, all delays are expressed in terms of time units. The association of time units with actual time is done using the `timescale compiler directive. This directive is used to specify the time unit and time precision. The directive is of the form:

```
`timescale time_unit / time_precision
```

where the *time_unit* and *time_precision* is made up of values from 1, 10, and 100 and units from s, ms, us, ns, ps and fs. Here is an example.

```
`timescale 1ns / 100ps
```

indicates a time unit of 1ns and a time precision of 100ps. The `timescale directive appears outside of a module declaration and affects all delay values that follow it. Here is an example.

```
`timescale 1ns / 100ps
module AndFunc (Z, A, B);
  output Z;
  input A, B;

  and #(5.22, 6.17) A1 (Z, A, B);
    // Rise and fall delay specified.
endmodule
```

The directive specifies all delays to be in ns and delays are rounded to one-tenth of a ns (100ps). Therefore, the delay value 5.22 becomes 5.2ns and the delay value 6.17 becomes 6.2ns. If instead the following `timescale directive is used in the above module,

```
`timescale 10ns / 1ns
```

then 5.22 becomes 52ns, and 6.17 becomes 62ns.

The `timescale directive affects all delays in modules that follow this directive in a compilation until another `timescale directive or `resetall directive is found. What happens if there is more than one module in a design each having its own `timescale directive? In such a case, simulation always takes place in the smallest time precision of all the modules and all delays are appropriately scaled to this smallest time precision. Here is an example.

```
`timescale 1ns / 100ps
module AndFunc (Z, A, B);
  output Z;
  input A, B;

  and #(5.22, 6.17) A1 (Z, A, B);
endmodule

`timescale 10ns / 1ns
module TB;
  reg PutA, PutB;
  wire GetO;

  initial
    begin
      PutA = 0;
      PutB = 0;
      #5.21 PutB = 1;
      #10.4 PutA = 1;
      #15 PutB = 0;
    end

  AndFunc AF1 (GetO, PutA, PutB);
endmodule
```

In this example, each module has its own `timescale directive. The `timescale directive is first applied to the delays. Therefore in the first module, 5.22 is 5.2ns, 6.17 is 6.2ns, and in the second module, 5.21 is 52ns, 10.4 is 104ns, and 15 is 150ns. If module *TB* were simulated, the smallest time precision of all modules in this design is 100ps. Therefore, all delays (especially the delays in module *TB*) will be scaled to a precision of 100ps. Delay 52ns now becomes 520*100ps, 104ns becomes 1040*100ps, and 150ns becomes 1500*100ps. More importantly, simulation occurs using a time precision of 100ps. If module *AndFunc* were simulated, the `timescale directive of module *TB* has no effect since module *TB* is not a child module of module *AndFunc*.

3.5.7   `unconnected_drive and `nounconnected_drive

Any unconnected input ports in module instantiations that appear between these two directives are either pulled up or pulled down.

```
`unconnected_drive pull1
. . .
/* All unconnected input ports between these two directives
   are pulled up (connected to 1). */
`nounconnected_drive


`unconnected_drive pull0
. . .
/* All unconnected input ports between these two directives
   are pulled down (connected to 0). */
`nounconnected_drive
```

3.5.8   `celldefine and `endcelldefine

These two directives are used to mark a module as a cell module. They typically encompass a module definition, as shown in the following example.

```
`celldefine
module FD1S3AX (D, CK, Z);

   . . .

endmodule
`endcelldefine
```

Cell modules are used by some PLI routines.

3.6   Value Set

Verilog HDL has the following four basic values.

    i.   **0** : logic-0 or false

    ii. **1** : logic-1 or true

    iii. **x** : unknown

    iv. **z** : high-impedance

Note that the interpretations of these four values are built-in into the language. A **z** in a value always means a high-impedance, a 0 always means a logic-0, and so on.

A **z** value at the input of a gate or in an expression is usually interpreted as an **x**. Furthermore, the values **x** and **z** are case-insensitive, that is, the value 0x1z is same as 0X1Z. A constant in Verilog HDL is made up of the above four basic values.

There are three types of constants in Verilog HDL.

    i.   Integer

    ii. Real

    iii. String

An underscore (_) character can be used in an integer or a real constant freely; they are ignored in the number itself. They can be used to improve readability; the only restriction is that the underscore character cannot be the first character.

3.6.1   Integers

An integer number can be written in the following two forms.

    i.   Simple decimal

    ii. Base format

Simple Decimal Form

An integer in this form is specified as a sequence of digits with an optional + (unary) or a − (unary) operator. Here are some examples of integers in the simple decimal form.

```
32        is decimal 32
- 15      is decimal -15
```

An integer value in this form represents a signed number. A negative number is represented in two's complement form. Thus 32 is 10000 in a 5-bit binary, 010000 in 6-bit binary; −15 is 10001 in 5-bit binary, and is 110001 in a 6-bit binary.

Base Format Notation

The format of an integer in this form is:

```
[ size ] 'base value
```

where the *size* specifies the size of the constant in number of bits, *base* is one of o or O (for octal), b or B (for binary), d or D (for decimal), h or H (for hexadecimal) and *value* is a sequence of digits that are values from the *base*. The values x and z and the hexadecimal values a through f are case-insensitive.

Here are some examples.

```
5'O37      5-bit octal
4'D2       4-bit decimal
4'B1x_01   4-bit binary
7'Hx       7-bit x (x extended), that is, xxxxxxx
4'hZ       4-bit z (z extended), that is, zzzz
4'd-4      Not legal: value cannot be negative
8 'h 2A    Spaces are allowed between size and ' character
           and between base and value
3' b001    Not legal: no space allowed between ' and base b
(2+3)'d10  Not legal; size cannot be an expression
```

Note that an x (or z) in a hexadecimal value represents four bits of x (or z), x (or z) in octal represents three bits of x (or z), and x (or z) in binary represents one bit of x (or z).

A number in base format notation is always an unsigned number. The size specification is optional in an integer of this form. If no size is specified in an integer, the size of the number is the number of bits specified in the value. Here are some examples.

```
'o721       9-bit octal
'hAF        8-bit hex
```

If the size specified is larger than the size specified for the constant, the number is padded to the left with 0's except for the case where the leftmost bit is a x or a z, in which case a x or a z respectively is used to pad to the left. For example,

```
10'b10      Padded with 0 to the left, 0000000010
10'bx0x1    Padded with x to the left, xxxxxxx0x1
```

If the size specified is smaller, then the leftmost bits are appropriately truncated. For example,

```
3'b1001_0011     is same as 3'b011
5'H0FFF          is same as 5'H1F
```

The ? character can be used as an alternate for value z in a number. It may be used to improve readability in cases where the value z is interpreted as a don't-care value (see Chapter 8).

3.6.2   Reals

A real number can be specified in one of the following two forms.

i. Decimal notation: Examples of numbers in this form are:

```
2.0
5.678
11572.12
0.1
```

```
2.        // Not legal: must have a digit
          // on either side of decimal.
```

ii. Scientific notation: Examples of numbers in this form are:

```
23_5.1e2    The value 23510.0; underscores are ignored
3.6E2       360.0 (e is same as E)
5E-4        0.0005
```

Implicit conversion to integer is defined by the language. Real numbers are converted to integers by rounding to the nearest integer.

```
42.446, 42.45 when converted to integer yields 42
92.5, 92.699  yield 93 when converted into integer
-15.62        to integer gives -16
-26.22        to integer gives -26
```

3.6.3   Strings

A string is a sequence of characters within double quotes. A string may not be split across lines. Here are examples of strings.

```
"INTERNAL ERROR"
"REACHED->HERE"
```

A character is represented by an 8-bit ASCII value which is treated as an unsigned integer. Therefore a string is a sequence of 8-bit ASCII values. To store the string "INTERNAL ERROR", a variable of size 8*14 is needed.

```
reg [ 1 : 8*14 ] Message;
. . .
Message = "INTERNAL ERROR";
```

The \ (backslash) character can be used to escape certain special characters.

```
\n      newline character
\t      tab
\\      the \ character itself
```

```
\"      the " character
\206    character with octal value 206
```

3.7   Data Types

Verilog HDL has two groups of data types.

i. **Net type**:

A *net type* represents a physical connection between structural elements. Its value is determined from the value of its drivers such as a continuous assignment or a gate output. If no driver is connected to a net, the net defaults to a value of **z**.

ii. **Register type**:

A *register type* represents an abstract data storage element. It is assigned values only within an always statement or an initial statement, and its value is saved from one assignment to the next. A register type has a default value of **x**.

3.7.1   Net Types

Here are the different kinds of nets that belong to the net data type.

- wire
- tri
- wor
- trior
- wand
- triand
- trireg
- tri1
- tri0
- supply0
- supply1

A simple syntax for a net declaration is:

net_kind [*msb* : *lsb*] *net1, net2 , ... , netN ;*

where *net_kind* is one of the nets listed above. *msb* and *lsb* are constant expressions that specify the range of the net; the range specification is optional; if no range is specified, a net defaults to a size of one bit. Here are some examples of net declarations.

```
wire Rdy, Start;  // Two 1-bit wire nets.
wand [2:0] Addr;  // Addr is a 3-bit vector wand net.
```

The various nets behave differently when there exists more than one driver for a net, that is, when there are multiple assignments to a net. For example,

```
wor Rde;
. . .
assign Rde = Blt & Wyl;
. . .
assign Rde = Kbl | Kip;
```

In this example, *Rde* has two drivers, one from each of the continuous assignments. Since it is a wor net, the effective value of *Rde* is determined from a wor table (see following section on wor nets) using the values of the drivers (the values of the right-hand side expressions).

Wire and Tri Nets

This is the most common type of net which is used to connect elements. A wire net and a tri net are identical in syntax and semantics; the tri net may be used to describe a net where multiple drivers drive a net, and has no other special significance.

```
wire Reset;
wire [3:2] Cla, Pla, Sla;
tri [MSB-1 : LSB+1] Art;
```

If multiple drivers drive a wire (or a tri) net, the effective value of the net is determined by using the following table.

wire (or tri)	0	1	x	z
0	0	x	x	0

wire (or tri)	0	1	x	z
1	x	1	x	1
x	x	x	x	x
z	0	1	x	z

Here is an example.

```
assign Cla = Pla & Sla;
. . .
assign Cla = Pla ^ Sla;
```

In this example, *Cla* has two drivers. The values of the two drivers (the values of the right-hand side expressions) is used to index in the above table to determine the effective value of *Cla*. Since *Cla* is a vector, each bit position is evaluated independently. For example, if the first right-hand side expression has the value **01x** and the second right-hand side expression has the value **11z**, the effective value of *Cla* is **x1x** (the first bits 0 and 1 index into the table to give an **x**, the second bits 1 and 1 index into the table to give a 1, the third bits **x** and **z** index into the table to give an **x**).

Wor and Trior Nets

This is a wired-or net, that is, if any one of the drivers is a 1, the value on the net is also a 1. Both wor and trior nets are identical in their syntax and functionality.

```
wor   [MSB : LSB] Art;
trior [MAX-1 : MIN-1] Rdx, Sdx, Bdx;
```

If multiple drivers drive this net, the effective value of the net is determined by using the following table.

wor (or trior)	0	1	x	z
0	0	1	x	0

wor (or trior)	0	1	x	z
1	1	1	1	1
x	x	1	x	x
z	0	1	x	z

Wand and Triand Nets

This net is a wired-and net, that is, if any of the drivers is a 0, the value of the net is a 0. Both wand and triand nets are identical in their syntax and functionality.

```
wand [-7:0] Dbus;
triand Reset, Clk;
```

If multiple drivers drive a wand net, the following table is used to determine the effective value.

wand (or triand)	0	1	x	z
0	0	0	0	0
1	0	1	x	1
x	0	x	x	x
z	0	1	x	z

Trireg Net

This net stores a value (like a register) and is used to model a capacitive node. When all drivers to a trireg net are at high-impedance, that is, have the value z, the trireg net retains the last value on the net. In addition, the default initial value for a trireg net is an x.

```
trireg [1:8] Dbus, Abus;
```

Tri0 and Tri1 Nets

These nets also model wired-logic nets, that is, a net with more than one driver. The particular characteristic of a tri0 (tri1) net is that if no driver is driving this net, its value is 0 (1 for tri1).

```
tri0 [-3:3] GndBus;
tri1 [0:-5] OtBus, ItBus;
```

The following table shows the effective value for a tri0 or a tri1 net that has more than one driver.

tri0 (tri1)	0	1	x	z
0	0	x	x	0
1	x	1	x	1
x	x	x	x	x
z	0	1	x	0(1)

Supply0 and Supply1 Nets

The supply0 net is used to model ground, that is, the value 0, and the supply1 net is used to model a power net, that is, the value 1.

```
supply0 Gnd, ClkGnd;
supply1 [2:0] Vcc;
```

3.7.2   Undeclared Nets

In Verilog HDL, it is possible not to declare a net. In such a case, the net defaults to a 1-bit wire net.

This implicit net declaration can be changed by using the `default_nettype compiler directive. It is of the form:

```
`default_nettype net_kind
```

For example, with the compiler directive:

```
`default_nettype wand
```

any undeclared net defaults to a 1-bit wand net.

3.7.3   Vectored and Scalared Nets

The keywords, **scalared** or **vectored**, can optionally be specified for a vector net. If a net is declared with the keyword **vectored**, then bit-selects and part-selects of this vector net are not allowed; in other words, the entire net has to be assigned (bit-selects and part-selects are described in the next chapter). Here is an example of such a declaration.

```
wire vectored [3:1] Grb;
    // Bit-select Grb[2] and part-select Grb[3:2]
    // are NOT allowed.

wor scalared [4:0] Best;
    // Same as:
    // wor [4:0] Best;
    // Bit-select Best[2] and part-select Best[3:1]
    // are allowed.
```

If no such keyword is specified, then the default is **scalared**.

3.7.4   Register Types

There are five different kinds of register types.
* reg
* integer
* time
* real
* realtime

Reg Register

The reg kind of register data type is the one most commonly used. A reg is declared by using a reg declaration, which is of the form:

```
reg [ msb : lsb ] reg1 , reg2 , . . . , regN ;
```

where *msb* and *lsb* specify the range and are constant-valued expressions. The range specification is optional; if no range is specified, it defaults to a 1-bit register. Here are some examples.

```
reg [3:0] Sat;          // Sat is a 4-bit register.
reg Cnt;                // A 1-bit register.
reg [1:32] Kisp, Pisp, Lisp;
```

A register can be of any size. A value in a register is always interpreted as an unsigned number.

```
reg [1:4] Comb;
. . .
Comb = -2; // Comb has 14 (1110), the two's complement of 2.
Comb = 5;  // Comb has 5 (0101).
```

Memories

A *memory* is an array of registers. It is declared using a reg declaration of the form:

```
reg [ msb : lsb ]  memory1 [upper1 : lower1 ],
                   memory2 [upper2 : lower2 ], . . . ;
```

Here is an example of a memory declaration.

```
reg [0:3] MyMem [0:63];
  // MyMem is an array of sixty-four 4-bit registers.
reg Bog[1:5];
  // Bog is an array of five 1-bit registers.
```

MyMem and *Bog* are memories. Arrays with more than two dimensions are not allowed. Notice that a memory belongs to the register data type. There is no such equivalent for the net data type.

A single reg declaration can be used to declare both registers and memories.

```
parameter ADDR_SIZE = 16, WORD_SIZE = 8;
reg [1:WORD_SIZE] RamPar [ADDR_SIZE-1 : 0], DataReg;
```

RamPar is a memory, an array of sixteen 8-bit registers, while *DataReg* is a 8-bit register.

A word of caution in assignments. A memory cannot be assigned a value in one assignment, but a register can. Therefore an index needs to be specified for a memory when it is being assigned. Let's look at this difference. In the following assignment,

```
reg [1:5] Dig;   // Dig is a 5-bit register.
. . .
Dig = 5'b11011;
```

is okay, but the following assignment:

```
reg Bog [1:5];   // Bog is a memory of five 1-bit registers.
. . .
Bog = 5'b11011;
```

is not. One way to assign to a memory is to assign a value to each word of a memory individually. For example,

```
reg [0:3] Xrom [1:4];
. . .
Xrom[1] = 4'hA;
Xrom[2] = 4'h8;
Xrom[3] = 4'hF;
Xrom[4] = 4'h2;
```

An alternate way to assign values to a memory is by using the system tasks:

i.   **$readmemb** (loads binary values)

ii. **$readmemh** (loads hexadecimal values)

These system tasks read and load data from a specified text file into a memory. The text file must contain the appropriate form of numbers, either binary or hexadecimal. Here is an example.

```
reg [1:4] RomB [7:1];
$readmemb ("ram.patt", RomB);
```

RomB is a memory. The file "ram.patt" must contain binary values. The file may also contain white spaces and comments. Here is an example of what may be in the file.

```
1101
1100
1000
0111
0000
1001
0011
```

The system task **$readmemb** causes the values to be read in starting from index 7, the leftmost word index of *RomB*. If only a part of the memory is to be loaded, the range can be explicitly specified in the **$readmemb** task, such as:

```
$readmemb ("ram.patt", RomB, 5, 3);
```

in which case only *RomB*[5], *RomB*[4], and *RomB*[3] words are read from the file beginning at the top. The values read are 1101, 1100 and 1000.

The file may also contain explicit addresses of the form:

```
@hex_address  value
```

such as in this example:

```
@5    11001
@2    11010
```

in which case the values are read into the specified addresses of the memory.

When only a start value is specified, read continues until the right-hand index bound of the memory is reached. For example,

```
$readmemb ("rom.patt", RomB, 6);
    // Starts from address 6 and continues until 1.
```

```
$readmemb ("rom.patt", RomB, 6, 4);
   // Reads from addresses 6 through 4.
```

Integer Register

An integer register contains integer values. It can be used as a general purpose register, typically for modeling high-level behavior. It is declared using an integer declaration of the form:

```
integer integer1 , integer2, . . . , integerN [ msb : lsb ];
```

msb and *lsb* are constant-valued expressions that specify the range of an integer array; the array range specification is optional. Notice that no bit range is allowed. An integer holds a minimum of 32 bits; however, an implementation may provide more. Here are some examples of integer declarations.

```
integer A, B, C;    // Three integer registers.
integer Hist[3:6]; // An array of four integers.
```

An integer register holds signed quantities and arithmetic operations provide two's complement arithmetic results.

An integer cannot be accessed as a bit-vector. For example, given the above declaration for integer *B*, *B*[6] and *B*[20:10] are not allowed. One way to extract a bit-value of an integer is to assign it to a reg register and then select the bits from the reg register. Here is an example.

```
reg [31:0] Breg;
integer Bint;
. . .
// Bint[6] and Bint[20:10] are not allowed.
. . .
Breg = Bint;
/* At this point, Breg[6] and Breg[20:10] are allowed and
   give the corresponding bit-values from the
   integer Bint */
```

This example shows that converting an integer to a bit-vector can be accomplished by simply using an assignment. Type conversion is automatic. No special functions are necessary. Converting from a bit-vector to an integer can also be accomplished by using an assignment. Here are some examples.

```
integer J;
reg [3:0] Bcq;

J = 6;          // J has the value 32'b0000...00110.
Bcq = J;        // Bcq has the value 4'b0110.

Bcq = 4'b0101;
J = Bcq;        /// J has value 32'b0000...00101.

J = -6;         // J has the value 32'b1111...11010.
Bcq = J;        // Bcq has the value 4'b1010.
```

Note that the assignment always takes place from the rightmost bit to the leftmost bit; any extra bits are truncated. It is easy to think of type conversion if you can remember that integers are represented as two's complement bit-vectors.

Time Register

A time register is used to store and manipulate time values. It is declared using a time declaration of the form:

```
time time_id1 , time_id2 , . . ., time_idN [ msb : lsb ];
```

where *msb* and *lsb* are constant-valued expressions that indicate the range of indices. If no range is specified, each identifier stores one time value which is at least 64 bits. A time register holds only an unsigned quantity. Here are examples of time declarations.

```
time Events[0:31];   // Array of time values.
time CurrTime;       // CurrTime holds one time value.
```

Real and Realtime Register

A real register (or a realtime register) can be declared using the following form.

```
// Real declaration:
real real_reg1 , real_reg2 , . . . , real_regN ;
// Realtime declaration:
realtime realtime_reg1 , realtime_reg2 , . . . ,
        realtime_regN ;
```

A realtime register is exactly identical to a real register. Here are some examples.

```
real Swing, Top;
realtime CurrTime;
```

The default value of a real register is 0. No range, bit range or word range, is allowed for declaring a real register.

When assigning values **x** and **z** to a real register, these values are treated as a 0.

```
real RamCnt;
. . .
RamCnt = 'b01x1Z;
```

RamCnt has the value 'b01010 after the assignment.

3.8   Parameters

A *parameter* is a constant. It is often used to specify delays and widths of variables. A parameter can be assigned a value only once, using a parameter declaration. A parameter declaration is of the form:

```
parameter param1 = const_expr1 , param2 = const_exp2 , . . . ,
        paramN = const_exprN ;
```

Here are some examples.

```
parameter LINELENGTH = 132, ALL_X_S = 16'bx;
parameter BIT = 1, BYTE = 8, PI = 3.14;
```

```
parameter STROBE_DELAY = (BYTE + BIT) / 2;
parameter TQ_FILE = "/home/bhasker/TEST/add.tq";
```

A parameter value can also be changed at compile time. This is done by using a defparam statement or by specifying the parameter value in the module instantiation statement (these two mechanisms are described in Chapter 9).

3.9   Exercises

1. Identify the legal and illegal identifiers:
    *COunT, 1_2Many, **1 , Real?, \\wait , Initial*

2. What first character identifies a system task or a system function?

3. Explain the text substitution compiler directive using an example.

4. Is there a Boolean type in Verilog HDL?

5. What are the bit patterns for the following:
    7'o44, 'Bx0, 5'bx110, 'hA0, 10'd2, 'hzF

6. What is the bit pattern stored in *Qpr* after the assignment?

    ```
    reg [1 : 8*2] Qpr;
    . . .
    Qpr = "ME";
    ```

7. If a net *Bnq* is declared but no assignment is made to it, what is its default value?

8. Verilog HDL allows a net not to be explicitly declared. If so, how is the net kind determined?

9. What is wrong with the following?

    ```
    integer [0:3] Ripple;
    ```

10. Write a system task to load a 32 by 64 word memory from a data file "memA.data".

11. State two ways by which you can override a parameter value at compile time.

❏

Chapter 4

EXPRESSIONS

This chapter describes the basics of how expressions are formed in Verilog HDL.

An expression is formed using operands and operators. An expression can be used wherever a value is expected.

4.1   Operands

An operand can be one of the following.

i.   Constant
ii. Parameter
iii. Net
iv. Register
v.   Bit-select
vi. Part-select
vii. Memory element

viii. Function call

4.1.1   Constant

Constants were described in the previous chapter. Here are some examples.

```
256, 7              // Unsized decimal numbers
4'b10_11, 8'h0A // Sized integer constants
'b1, 'hFBA          // Unsized integer constants
90.00006            // Real constant
"BOND"              /* String constant; each character is stored
                       as a 8-bit ASCII value */
```

An integer value in an expression is interpreted as either a signed or an unsigned number. If it is a decimal integer, for example, 12, then it is interpreted as a signed number. If the integer is a based integer (unsized or sized), then it is treated as an unsigned number. Here are some examples.

```
12       is  01100 in 5-bit vector form (signed)
-12      is  10100 in 5-bit vector form (signed)
5'b01100 is  decimal 12 (unsigned)
5'b10100 is  decimal 20 (unsigned)
4'd12    is  decimal 12 (unsigned)
```

More important is the fact that a negative value of an integer is treated differently for an integer with or without a base. The negative value of an integer with no base specifier is treated as a signed value, while an integer with a base specifier is treated as an unsigned value. Thus, −44 is treated different from −6'o54 (decimal 44 is octal 54) as shown in the next example.

```
integer Cone;
. . .
Cone = - 44 / 4;
Cone = - 6'o54 / 4;
```

Note that both −44 and −6'o54 are evaluated to the same bit pattern; however −44 is treated as a signed number, while −6'o54 is treated as an unsigned number. Thus *Cone* in the first assignment has the value −11, while *Cone* has the value 1073741813 in the second assignment.

4.1.2   Parameter

Parameters were described in the previous chapter. A parameter is like a constant and is declared using a parameter declaration. Here is an example of a parameter declaration.

```
parameter LOAD = 4'd12, STORE = 4'd10;
```

LOAD and *STORE* are examples of parameters that are declared to have the values 12 and 10 respectively.

4.1.3   Net

Both scalar nets (1-bit) and vector nets (multi-bit) can be used in an expression. Here are examples of net declarations.

```
wire [0:3] Prt;    // Prt is a 4-bit vector net.
wire Bbq;          // Bbq is a scalar net.
```

A value in a net is interpreted as an unsigned value. In the continuous assignment,

```
assign Prt = - 3;
```

Prt has the bit-vector 1101 assigned which is in effect the decimal value 13. In the following continuous assignment,

```
assign Prt = 4'HA;
```

Prt has the bit-vector 1010 assigned to it which is the decimal value 10.

4.1.4   Register

Scalar and vector registers can be used in an expression. A register is declared using a register declaration. Here are some examples.

```
integer TemA, TemB;
reg [1:5] State;
time Que [1:5];
```

A value in an integer register is interpreted as a signed two's complement number while a value in a reg register or a time register is interpreted as an unsigned number. Values in real and realtime registers are interpreted as signed floating point values.

```
TemA = - 10;     // TemA has the bit-vector 10110, which
                 // is the two's complement of 10.
TemA = 'b1011;   // TemA has the decimal value 11.

State = - 10;    // State has the bit-vector 10110,
                 // which is decimal 22.
State = 'b1011;  // State has the bit-vector 01011,
                 // which is the decimal value 11.
```

4.1.5   Bit-select

A bit-select extracts a particular bit from a vector. It is of the form:

```
net_or_reg_vector [ bit_select_expr]
```

Here are examples of bit-selects used in expressions.

```
State[1] && State[4]     // Register bit-select
Prt[0] | Bbq             // Net bit-select
```

If the select expression evaluates to an x or a z or if it is out of bounds, the value of the bit-select is an x, for example, State[x] is an x.

4.1.6   Part-select

In a part-select, a contiguous sequence of bits of a vector is selected. It is of the form:

```
net_or_reg_vector [ msb_const_expr :lsb_const_expr]
```

where the range expressions must be constant expressions. Here are some examples.

```
State [1:4]        // Register part-select
Prt [1:3]          // Net part-select
```

If either of the range index is out of bounds or evaluates to an x or a z, the part-select value is an x.

4.1.7   Memory Element

A memory element selects one word of a memory. It is of the form:

```
memory[ word_address ]
```

Here is an example.

```
reg [1:8] Ack, Dram[0:63];
. . .
Ack = Dram[60];    // 60th element of memory.
```

No part-select or bit-select of a memory is allowed. For example,

```
Dram[60] [2]           is not allowed.
Dram[60] [2:4]         is also not allowed.
```

One approach to read a bit-select or a part-select of a word in memory is to assign the memory element to a register and then use a part-select or a bit-select of this register. For example, *Ack*[2] and *Ack*[2:4] are legal expressions.

4.1.8   Function Call

A function call can be used in an expression. It can either be a system function call (starts with the $ character) or a user-defined function call.

```
$time + SumOfEvents (A, B)
  /* $time is a system function and SumOfEvents is a
     user-defined function (defined elsewhere) */
```

Functions are described in greater detail in Chapter 10.

4.2   Operators

Operators in Verilog HDL are classified into the following categories.

i. Arithmetic operators

ii. Relational operators

iii. Equality operators

iv. Logical operators

v. Bitwise operators

vi. Reduction operators

vii. Shift operators

viii. Conditional operators

ix. Concatenation and replication operators

The following table shows the precedence and names of all the operators. The operators are listed from highest precedence (top row) to the lowest precedence (bottom row). Operators in the same row have identical precedence.

+	Unary plus
−	Unary minus
!	Unary logical negation
~	Unary bit-wise negation
&	Reduction and
~&	Reduction nand
^	Reduction xor
^~ or ~^	Reduction xnor
|	Reduction or
~|	Reduction nor
*	Multiply
/	Divide
%	Modulus
+	Binary plus
−	Binary minus

<<	Left shift
>>	Right shift
<	Less than
<=	Less than or equal to
>	Greater than
>=	Greater than or equal to
==	Logical equality
!=	Logical inequality
===	Case equality
!==	Case inequality
&	Bit-wise and
^	Bit-wise xor
^~ or ~^	Bit-wise xnor
|	Bit-wise or
&&	Logical and
||	Logical or
?:	Conditional operator

All operators associate left to right except for the conditional operator that associates right to left. The expression:

```
A + B - C
```

is evaluated as:

```
(A + B) - C          // Left to right
```

while the expression:

```
A ? B : C ? D : F
```

is evaluated as:

```
A ? B : (C ? D : F )    // Right to left.
```

Parentheses can be used to change the order of precedence, such as in the expression:

$(A \ ? \ B \ : \ C) \ ? \ D \ : \ F$

4.2.1 Arithmetic Operators

The arithmetic operators are:
- + (unary and binary plus)
- − (unary and binary minus)
- * (multiply)
- / (divide)
- % (modulus)

Integer division truncates any fractional part. For example,

```
7 / 4            is 1
```

The % (modulus) operator gives the remainder with the sign of the first operand.

```
7 % 4            is 3
```

while:

```
-7 % 4           is -3
```

If any bit of an operand in an arithmetic operation is an **x** or a **z**, the entire result is an **x**. For example,

```
'b10x1 + 'b01111    is  'bxxxxx
```

Result Size

The size of the result of an arithmetic expression is determined by the size of the largest operand. In case of an assignment, it is determined by the size of the left-hand side target as well. Consider the following example.

```
reg [0:3] Arc, Bar, Crt;
reg [0:5] Frx;
. . .
Arc = Bar + Crt;
Frx = Bar + Crt;
```

The result size of the first addition is determined by the size of *Bar*, *Crt* and *Arc* which is four bits. The size of the second addition operation is decided similarly by the size of *Frx* (largest of sizes *Frx*, *Bar*, *Crt*), which is six bits. So in the first assignment, any overflow from the plus operation is discarded while in the second assignment, any overflow bit is saved in the result bit *Frx*[1].

In larger expressions, how are the sizes of the intermediate results determined? Verilog HDL defines a rule which states that all intermediate results of an expression shall take the size of the largest operand (in case of an assignment, this also includes the left-hand side target). Consider another example.

```
wire [4:1] Box, Drt;
wire [1:5] Cfg;
wire [1:6] Peg;
wire [1:8] Adt;
. . .
assign Adt = (Box + Cfg) + (Drt + Peg);
```

The size of the largest operand in the right-hand side expression is 6, but including the size of the left-hand side, the largest size is 8. So all additions are performed using 8 bits. For example, adding *Box* and *Cfg* yields a result of size 8.

Unsigned and Signed

When performing arithmetic operations and assignments, it is important to note which operands are being treated as unsigned values and which are being treated as signed values. An unsigned value is stored in:

- a net
- a reg register
- an integer in base format notation

A signed value is stored in:

- an integer register
- an integer in decimal form

Here are some examples of assignments.

```
reg [0:5] Bar;
integer Tab;
. . .
Bar = - 4'd12;      // Reg Bar has the decimal value 52,
                    // which is the vector 110100.
Tab = - 4'd12;      // Integer Tab has the value -12
                    // (bits 110100)

- 4'd12 / 4         // Result is 1073741821.
- 12 / 4            // Result is -3.
```

Since *Bar* is a reg register, it stores only unsigned values. The value of the right-hand side expression is 'b110100 (the two's complement of 12). Thus *Bar* holds the decimal value 52 after the assignment. In the second assignment, the right-hand side expression is the same, whose value is 'b110100, but this time it is being assigned to an integer register which holds signed quantities. Thus *Tab* holds the decimal value -12 (the bit-vector 110100). Note that in both cases, the same bit-vector is stored; however, in the first case, the vector is interpreted as an unsigned number and in the second case, it is interpreted as a signed number.

Here are some more examples.

```
Bar = - 4'd12 / 4;
Tab = - 4'd12 / 4;

Bar = - 12 / 4;
Tab = - 12 / 4;
```

In the first assignment, *Bar* gets the decimal value 61 (bit-vector 111101), while in the second assignment, *Tab* gets the decimal value 1073741821 (bit-vector 0011...11101). *Bar* gets the same value in the third assignment as in the first assignment. This is because *Bar* holds only unsigned values. In the fourth assignment, *Tab* gets the decimal value -3.

Here are some more examples.

```
Bar = 4 - 6;
Tab = 4 - 6;
```

Bar gets the decimal value 62 (two's complement of −2), while *Tab* gets the decimal value −2 (bit-vector 111110).

Here is another example.

```
Bar = -2 + (-4);
Tab = -2 + (-4);
```

Bar gets the decimal value 58 (bit-vector 111010), while *Tab* gets the decimal value −6 (bit-vector 111010).

4.2.2   Relational Operators

The relational operators are:
- > (greater than)
- < (less than)
- >= (greater than or equal to)
- <= (less than or equal to)

The result of a relational operator is true (the value 1) or false (the value 0). Result is an x if any bit in either of the operands is an x or a z. For example,

```
23 > 45
```

is false (value 0), while:

```
52 < 8'hxFF
```

is x. If operands are not of the same size, the smaller operand is zero-filled on the most significant bit side (the left). For example,

```
'b1000 >= 'b01110
```

is equivalent to:

```
'b01000 >= 'b01110
```

which is false (value 0).

4.2.3   Equality Operators

The equality operators are:
- == (logical equality)
- != (logical inequality)
- === (case equality)
- !== (case inequality)

The result is 0 if the comparison is false, else the result is a 1. In case comparisons, values x and z are compared strictly as values, that is, with no interpretations, and the result can never be an unknown, while in logical comparisons, values x and z have their usual meaning and the result may be unknown; that is, for logical comparisons if either operand contains an x or a z, the result is the unknown value (x).

Here is an example. Given:

```
Data = 'b11x0;
Addr = 'b11x0;
```

then:

```
Data == Addr
```

is unknown, that is, the value x, and:

```
Data === Addr
```

is true, that is, the value 1.

If the operands are of unequal lengths, the smaller operand is zero-filled on the most significant side, that is, on the left. For example,

```
2'b10 == 4'b0010
```

is same as:

```
4'b0010 == 4'b0010
```

which is true (the value 1).

4.2.4   Logical Operators

The logical operators are:

- && (logical and)
- || (logical or)
- ! (unary logical negation)

These operators operate on logical values 0 or 1. The result of a logical operation is a 0 or a 1. For example, given:

```
Crd = 'b0;   // 0 is false.
Dgs = 'b1;   // 1 is true.
```

then:

```
Crd && Dgs      is 0 (false)
Crd || Dgs      is 1 (true)
! Dgs           is 0 (false)
```

For vector operands, a non-zero vector is treated as a 1. For example, given:

```
A_Bus = 'b0110;
B_Bus = 'b0100;
```

then:

```
A_Bus || B_Bus      is 1
A_Bus && B_Bus      is also 1
```

and:

```
! A_Bus    is same as  ! B_Bus
```

which is 0.

If a bit in any of the operands is an x, the result is also an x.

```
!x      is  x
```

4.2.5   Bit-wise Operators

The bit-wise operators are:
- ~ (unary negation)
- & (binary and)
- | (binary or)
- ^ (binary exclusive-or)
- ~^, ^~ (binary exclusive-nor)

These operators operate bit-by-bit, on corresponding bits of the input operands and produce a vector result. The following tables show the result of the bit-by-bit operation for the various operators.

& (and)	0	1	x	z
0	0	0	0	0
1	0	1	x	x
x	0	x	x	x
z	0	x	x	x

| (or)	0	1	x	z
0	0	1	x	x
1	1	1	1	1
x	x	1	x	x
z	x	1	x	x

^ (xor)	0	1	x	z
0	0	1	x	x
1	1	0	x	x
x	x	x	x	x
z	x	x	x	x

^~ (xnor)	0	1	x	z
0	1	0	x	x
1	0	1	x	x
x	x	x	x	x
z	x	x	x	x

~ (negation)	0	1	x	z
	1	0	x	x

Here is an example. Given,

```
A = 'b0110;
B = 'b0100;
```

then:

```
A | B        is  0110
A & B        is  0100
```

If the operands are unequal in length, the smaller operand is zero-filled on the most significant side. For example,

```
'b0110 ^ 'b10000
```

is same as:

```
'b00110 ^ 'b10000
```

which is 'b10110.

4.2.6   Reduction Operators

The reduction operators operate on all bits of a single operand and produce a 1-bit result. The operators are:

- & (reduction and):
  If any bit is 0, the result is 0, else if any bit is an x or a z, the result is an x, else the result is a 1.
- ~& (reduction nand):
  Invert of & reduction operator.
- | (reduction or):
  If any bit is a 1, the result is 1, else if any bit is an x or a z, the result is an x, else the result is 0.
- ~| (reduction nor):
  Invert of | reduction operator.
- ^ (reduction xor):
  If any bit is an x or a z, the result is an x, else if there are even number of 1's in the operand, the result is 0, else the result is 1.
- ~^ (reduction xnor):
  Invert of ^ reduction operator.

Here are some examples. Given,

```
A = 'b0110;
B = 'b0100;
```

then:

```
| B          is 1
& B          is 0
~^ A         is 1
```

The reduction xor operator can be used to determine if any bit of a vector is an x. Given,

```
MyReg = 4'b01x0;
```

then:

^MyReg is an **x**

This can be checked using an if statement such as:

```
if (^MyReg === 1'bx)
    $display ("There is an unknown in the vector MyReg!");
```

Note that the logical equality (==) operator cannot be used for comparison; the logical equality operator comparison will only yield the result **x**. The case equality operator yields the value 1 which is the desired result.

4.2.7   Shift Operators

The shift operators are:

- << (left-shift)
- >> (right-shift)

The shift operation shifts the left operand by the right operand number of times. It is a logical shift. The vacated bits are filled with 0. If the right operand evaluates to an **x** or a **z**, the result of the shift operation is an **x**. Here is an example. Given:

```
reg [0:7] Qreg;
. . .
Qreg = 4'b0111;
```

then:

```
Qreg >> 2          is 8'b0000_0001
```

Verilog HDL has no exponentiation operator. However, the shift operator can be used to support this partly. For example, if you are interested in computing $2^{NumBits}$, this can be achieved by using the shift operator, such as:

```
32'b1 << NumBits          // NumBits must be less than 32.
```

In a similar vein, a 2-to-4 decoder can be modeled using a shift operator.

```
wire [0:3] DecodeOut = 4'd1 << Address[0:1];
```

Address[0:1] can have values 0, 1, 2, and 3. Correspondingly, *DecodeOut* has the values 4'b0001, 4'b0010, 4'b0100, and 4'b1000, thereby modeling a decoder.

4.2.8   Conditional Operator

The conditional operator selects an expression based on the value of the condition expression and it is of the form:

```
cond_expr ? expr1 : expr2
```

If *cond_expr* is true (that is, has value 1), *expr1* is selected, if *cond_expr* is false (value 0), *expr2* is selected. If *cond_expr* is an x or a z, the result is a bitwise operation on *expr1* and *expr2* with the following logic: 0 with 0 gives 0, 1 with 1 gives 1, rest are x.

Here is an example.

```
wire [0:2] Student = Marks > 18 ? Grade_A : Grade_C;
```

The expression *Marks* > 18 is computed; if true, *Grade_A* is assigned to *Student*, if *Marks* is <= 18, *Grade_C* is assigned to *Student*.

Here is another example.

```
always
    #5 Ctr = (Ctr != 25) ? (Ctr + 1) : 5;
```

The expression in the procedural assignment says that if *Ctr* is not equal to 25, increment *Ctr*, else if *Ctr* becomes 25, reset it to 5.

4.2.9   Concatenation and Replication

Concatenation is the operation of joining bits from smaller expressions to form larger expressions. It is of the form:

```
{ expr1 , expr2 , . . . , exprN }
```

Here are some examples.

```
wire [7:0] Dbus;
wire [11:0] Abus;


assign Dbus[7:4] = {Dbus[0], Dbus[1], Dbus[2], Dbus[3]};
          // Assign lower four bits in reverse order to upper
          // four bits.
assign Dbus = {Dbus[3:0], Dbus[7:4]};
          // Swap lower and upper four bits.
```

Concatenation of unsized constant numbers is not allowed as the size of these numbers are not known. For example,

```
{Dbus, 5}      // Unsized constant in concatenation is not
               // allowed.
```

is not legal.

Replication is performed by specifying a repetition number. It is of the form:

```
{ repetition_number { expr1 , expr2 ,. . . , exprN }}
```

Here are some examples.

```
Abus = {3{4'b1011}};   // The bit-vector 12'b1011_1011_1011
Abus = {{4 {Dbus[7]}}, Dbus}; /* Sign extension */

{3{1'b1}}    is 111
{3{Ack}}     is same as {Ack, Ack, Ack}
```

4.3   Kinds of Expressions

A *constant expression* is an expression that evaluates to a constant value at compile time. More specifically, a constant expression can be made up of:

    i.   constant literals, such as 'b10 and 326

    ii. parameter names, such as *RED* from the parameter declaration:

```
parameter RED = 4'b1110;
```

A *scalar expression* is an expression that evaluates to a 1-bit result. If a scalar result is expected but the expression produces a vector result, the least significant bit of the vector is used (the rightmost bit).

4.4   Exercises

1. Declare a parameter *GATE_DELAY* with a value of 5.

2. Given a memory of size 64 words, with 8 bits per word, write Verilog code to swap the contents of memory in reverse order, that is, transfer word at 0 to word at 63, word 1 to word 62, and so on.

3. Given a 32-bit bus, *Address_Bus*, write an expression that computes the reduction nand of bits 11 through 20.

4. Given one bus, *Control_Bus*[15:0], write an assignment statement that will split the bus into two buses, *Abus*[0:9] and *Bbus*[6:1].

5. Write an expression that performs the arithmetic shift of a 8-bit signed number contained in *Qparity*.

6. Using a conditional operator, write an assignment statement that selects the value of *NextState*. If *CurrentState* is *RESET*, then *NextState* is *GO*, if *CurrentState* is *GO*, *NextState* is *BUSY*, if *CurrentState* is *BUSY*, *NextState* is *RESET*.

7. Model the behavior of the 2-to-4 decoder circuit shown in Figure 2-2 using a single continuous assignment statement. [Hint: Use shift operator, conditional operator and the concatenation operator].

8. How would you generate a bus, *BusQ*[0:3], from four scalar variables, *A*, *B*, *C*, and *D*?
    How would you form a new bus, *BusR*[10:1], from two buses, *BusA*[0:3] and *BusY*[20:15]?

❏

Chapter 5

GATE-LEVEL MODELING

This chapter describes the gate-level modeling capability of Verilog HDL. It describes the available built-in primitive gates and how these can be used to describe hardware.

5.1 The Built-in Primitive Gates

The following built-in primitive gates are available in Verilog HDL.

i. Multiple-input gates:
and, nand, or, nor, xor, xnor

ii. Multiple-output gates:
buf, not

iii. Tristate gates:
bufif0, bufif1, notif0, notif1

iv. Pull gates:
pullup, pulldown

v. MOS switches:
cmos, nmos, pmos, rcmos, rnmos, rpmos

vi. Bidirectional switches:
tran, tranif0, tranif1, rtran, rtranif0, rtranif1

A gate can be used in a design using a gate instantiation. Here is a simple format of a gate instantiation.

```
gate_type [ instance_name ] ( term1 , term2 , . . . , termN ) ;
```

Note that the *instance_name* is optional; *gate_type* is one the gates listed earlier. The *term*s specify the nets and registers connected to the terminals of the gate.

Multiple instances of the same gate type can be specified in one construct. The syntax for this is the following.

```
gate_type
        [ instance_name1 ] ( term11 , term12 , . . . , term1N ),
        [ instance_name2 ] ( term21 , term22,. . . , term2N ),
        . . .
        [ instance_nameM ] ( termM1 , termM2 , . . . , termMN );
```

5.2   Multiple-input Gates

The multiple-input built-in gates are:

and   nand   nor   or   xor   xnor

These logic gates have only one output and one or more inputs. Here is the syntax of a multiple-input gate instantiation.

```
multiple_input_gate_type
    [ instance_name ] ( OutputA , Input1 , Input2 ,. . ., InputN );
```

The first terminal is the output and all others are the inputs. See Figure 5-1.

Here are some examples. The logic diagrams are shown in Figure 5-2.

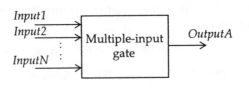

Figure 5-1 Multiple-input gate.

and *A1* (*Out1*, *In1*, *In2*);

and *RBX* (*Sty*, *Rib*, *Bro*, *Qit*, *Fix*);

xor (*Bar*, *Bud*[0], *Bud*[1], *Bud*[2]),
     (*Car*, *Cut*[0], *Cut*[1]),
     (*Sar*, *Sut*[2], *Sut*[1], *Sut*[0], *Sut*[3]);

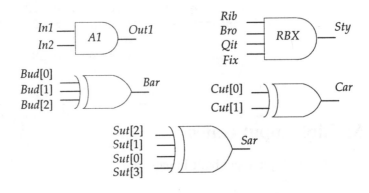

Figure 5-2 Multiple-input gate examples.

The first gate instantiation is a 2-input and gate with instance name *A1*, output *Out1* and with two inputs, *In1* and *In2*. The second gate instantiation is a 4-input and gate with instance name *RBX*, output *Sty* and four inputs, *Rib*, *Bro*, *Qit* and *Fix*. The third gate instantiation is an example of an xor gate with no instance name. Its output is *Bar* and it has three inputs, *Bud*[0], *Bud*[1] and *Bud*[2]. Also, this instantiation has two additional instances of the same type.

The truth tables for these gates are shown next. Notice that a value z at an input is handled like an x; additionally, the output of a multiple-input gate can never be a z.

nand	0	1	x	z
0	1	1	1	1
1	1	0	x	x
x	1	x	x	x
z	1	x	x	x

and	0	1	x	z
0	0	0	0	0
1	0	1	x	x
x	0	x	x	x
z	0	x	x	x

or	0	1	x	z
0	0	1	x	x
1	1	1	1	1
x	x	1	x	x
z	x	1	x	x

nor	0	1	x	z
0	1	0	x	x
1	0	0	0	0
x	x	0	x	x
z	x	0	x	x

xor	0	1	x	z
0	0	1	x	x
1	1	0	x	x
x	x	x	x	x
z	x	x	x	x

xnor	0	1	x	z
0	1	0	x	x
1	0	1	x	x
x	x	x	x	x
z	x	x	x	x

5.3   Multiple-output Gates

The multiple-output gates are:

buf   **not**

These gates have only one input and one or more outputs. See Figure 5-3. The basic syntax for this gate instantiation is:

```
multiple_output_gate_type
        [ instance_name ] ( Out1 , Out2 , . . . , OutN , InputA );
```

The last terminal is the input, all remaining terminals are the outputs.

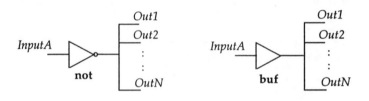

Figure 5-3   Multiple-output gates.

Here are some examples.

```
buf   B1  (Fan[0], Fan[1], Fan[2], Fan[3], Clk);
not   N1  (PhA, PhB, Ready);
```

In the first gate instance, *Clk* is the input to the buf gate; this gate instance has four outputs, *Fan*[0] through *Fan*[3]. In the second gate instance, *Ready* is the only input to the not gate. This instance has two outputs, *PhA* and *PhB*.

The truth table for these gates are shown next.

buf	0	1	x	z		not	0	1	x	z
(output)	0	1	x	x		(output)	1	0	x	x

5.4   Tristate Gates

The tristate gates are:

bufif0   bufif1   notif0   notif1

These gates model three-state drivers. These gates have one output, one data input and one control input. Here is the basic syntax of a tristate gate instantiation.

tristate_gate [*instance_name*] (*OutputA* , *InputB* , *ControlC*);

The first terminal *OutputA* is the output, the second terminal *InputB* is the data input, and the control input is *ControlC*. See Figure 5-4. Depending on the control input, the output can be driven to the high-impedance state, that is, to value **z**. For a bufif0 gate, the output is **z** if control is 1, else data is transferred to output. For a bufif1 gate, output is a **z** if control is 0. For a notif0 gate, output is at **z** if control is at 1 else output is the invert of the input data value. For notif1 gate, output is at **z** if control is at 0.

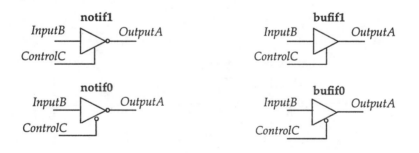

Figure 5-4   Tristate gates.

Here are some examples.

bufif1 *BF1* (*Dbus, MemData, Strobe*);
notif0 *NT2* (*Addr, Abus, Probe*);

The bufif1 gate *BF1* drives the output *Dbus* to high-impedance state when *Strobe* is 0, else *MemData* is transferred to *Dbus*. In the second instantiation, when *Probe* is 1, *Addr* is in high-impedance state, else *Addr* gets the inverted value of *Abus*.

The truth table for these gates are shown next. Some entries in the table indicate alternate entries. For example, 0/z indicates that the output can either be a 0 or a z depending on the strengths of the data and control values; strengths are discussed in Chapter 10.

bufif0		Control				**bufif1**		Control			
		0	1	x	z			0	1	x	z
	0	0	z	0/z	0/z		0	z	0	0/z	0/z
Data	1	1	z	1/z	1/z	Data	1	z	1	1/z	1/z
	x	x	z	x	x		x	z	x	x	x
	z	x	z	x	x		z	z	x	x	x

notif0		Control				**notif1**		Control			
		0	1	x	z			0	1	x	z
	0	1	z	1/z	1/z		0	z	1	1/z	1/z
Data	1	0	z	0/z	0/z	Data	1	z	0	0/z	0/z
	x	x	z	x	x		x	z	x	x	x
	z	x	z	x	x		z	z	x	x	x

5.5   Pull Gates

The pull gates are:

pullup   pulldown

These gates have only one output with no inputs. A pullup gate places a 1 on its output. A pulldown gate places a 0 on its output. A gate instantiation is of the form:

pull_gate [*instance_name*] (*OutputA*);

The terminal list of this gate instantiation contains only one output.

Here is an example.

pullup *PUP* (*Pwr*);

This pullup gate has instance name *PUP* with output *Pwr* tied to 1.

5.6   MOS Switches

The MOS switches are:

cmos   pmos   nmos   rcmos   rpmos   rnmos

These gates model unidirectional switches, that is, data flows from input to output and the data flow can be turned off by appropriately setting the control input(s).

The pmos (p-type MOS transistor), nmos (n-type MOS transistor), rnmos ('r' stands for resistive) and rpmos switches have one output, one input and one control input. The basic syntax for an instantiation is:

gate_type [*instance_name*] (*OutputA* , *InputB* , *ControlC*);

The first terminal is the output, the second terminal is the input and the last terminal is the control. If control is 0 for nmos and rnmos switches and 1 for pmos and rpmos switches, the switch is turned off, that is, output has value **z**; if control is 1, data at input passes to output; see Figure 5-5. The resistive switches (rnmos and rpmos) have a higher impedance (resistance) between the input and output terminals as compared to the non-resistive switches (nmos and pmos). Thus when data passes from input to output, a reduction in strength occurs for resistive switches; strengths are described in Chapter 10.

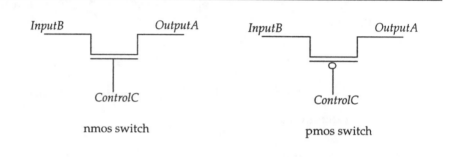

Figure 5-5   Nmos and pmos switches.

Here are some examples.

```
pmos P1 (BigBus, SmallBus, GateControl);
rnmos RN1 (ControlBit, ReadyBit, Hold);
```

The first instance instantiates a pmos switch with instance name *P1*. The input to the switch is *SmallBus* and the output is *BigBus* and the control signal is *GateControl*.

The truth tables for these switches are shown next. Some entries in the table indicate alternate entries. For example, 1/z indicates that the output can be either 1 or **z** depending on the input and control.

pmos rpmos		Control				nmos rnmos		Control			
		0	1	x	z			0	1	x	z
	0	0	z	0/z	0/z		0	z	0	0/z	0/z
Data	1	1	z	1/z	1/z	Data	1	z	1	1/z	1/z
	x	x	z	x	x		x	z	x	x	x
	z	z	z	z	z		z	z	z	z	z

The cmos (complimentary MOS) and rcmos (resistive version of cmos) switches have one data output, one data input and two control inputs. The syntax for instantiating these two switches is of the form:

```
(r)cmos  [ instance_name ]
                ( OutputA , InputB , NControl , PControl );
```

The first terminal is the output, the second is the input, the third is the n-channel control input and the fourth terminal is the p-channel control input. A cmos (rcmos) switch behaves exactly like a combination of a pmos (rpmos) and an nmos (rnmos) switch with common outputs and common inputs; see Figure 5-6.

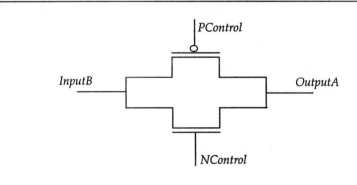

Figure 5-6 (r)cmos switch.

5.7   Bidirectional Switches

The bidirectional switches are:

tran rtran tranif0 rtranif0 tranif1 rtranif1

These switches are bidirectional, that is, data flows both ways and there is no delay when data propagates through the switches. The last four switches can be turned off by setting a control signal appropriately. The tran and rtran switches cannot be turned off.

The syntax for instantiating a tran or a rtran (resistive version of tran) switch is:

(r)tran [*instance_name*] (*SignalA* , *SignalB*);

The terminal list has only two terminals and data flows unconditionally both ways, that is, from *SignalA* to *SignalB* and vice versa.

The syntax for instantiating the other bidirectional switches is:

gate_type [*instance_name*] (*SignalA* , *SignalB* , *ControlC*);

The first two terminals are the bidirectional terminals, that is, data flows from *SignalA* to *SignalB* and vice versa. The third terminal is the control signal. If *ControlC* is 1 for tranif0 and rtranif0, and 0 for tranif1 and rtranif1, the bidirectional data flow is disabled. For the resistive switches (rtran, rtranif0 and rtranif1), the strength of the signal reduces when it passes through the switch; strengths are discussed in Chapter 10.

5.8   Gate Delays

The signal propagation delay from any gate input to the gate output can be specified using a *gate delay*. The gate delay can be specified in the gate instantiation itself. Here is the syntax of a gate instantiation with the delay specification.

gate_type [*delay*] [*instance_name*] (*terminal_list*);

The delay specifies the gate delay, that is, the propagation delay from any gate input to the output. When no gate delay is specified, the default delay is zero.

A gate delay can be comprised of up to three values:

i. rise delay

ii. fall delay

iii. turn-off delay

A delay specification may contain zero, one, two, or all three values specified. The following table shows the values that are used for a delay based on the number of specified values.

	No delay	1 value (d)	2 values (d1, d2)	3 values (dA, dB, dC)
Rise	0	d	d1	dA
Fall	0	d	d2	dB
To_x	0	d	min[a] (d1, d2)	min (dA, dB, dC)
Turn-off	0	d	min (d1, d2)	dC

a. min: minimum

Notice that the transition to x delay (to_x) cannot be explicitly specified but is determined from the other specified values.

Here are some examples. Note that all delays in a Verilog HDL model are expressed in terms of time units. The association of time units with actual time is done using the `timescale compiler directive. In the following instantiation,

not *N1* (*Qbar*, *Q*);

the gate delay is 0 since no delay has been specified. In the gate instantiation,

nand #6 (*Out*, *In1*, *In2*);

all delays are 6, that is, the rise delay and fall delay are both 6. Turn-off delay does not apply to a nand gate since the output never goes into high-impedance. The transition to x delay is also 6.

```
and #(3, 5) (Out, In1, In2, In3);
```

In this gate instantiation, the rise delay has been specified to be 3, the fall delay is 5 and the transition to x delay is the minimum of 3 and 5, which is 3. In the following gate instance,

```
notif1 #(2, 8, 6) (Dout, Din1, Din2);
```

the rise delay is 2, the fall delay is 8, the turn-off delay is 6 and the transition to x delay is the minimum of 2, 8 and 6, which is 2.

Multiple-input gates, such as **and** and **or**, and multiple-output gates (**buf** and **not**) can have only up to two delays specified (since output never goes to **z**). Tristate gates can have up to three delays and the pull gates cannot have any delays.

5.8.1   Min:typ:max Delay Form

A delay for a gate (including all other delays such as in continuous assignments) can also be specified in a *min:typ:max* form. The form is:

```
minimum : typical : maximum
```

The minimum, typical and maximum values must be constant expressions. Here is an example of a delay in this form used in a gate instantiation.

```
nand #(2:3:4, 5:6:7) (Pout, Pin1, Pin2);
```

The selection of which delay to use is usually made as an option during a simulation run. For example, if maximum delay simulation is performed, a rise delay of 4 and a fall delay of 7 is used for the nand gate instance.

A specify block can also be used to specify gate delays. Specify blocks are discussed in Chapter 10.

5.9   Array of Instances

When repetitive instances are required, a range specification can optionally be specified in a gate instantiation (a range specification can also be used in a module instantiation). The syntax of a gate instantiation in this case is:

> *gate_type* [*delay*] *instance_name* [*leftbound* : *rightbound*]
> (*list _of_ terminal_names*);

The *leftbound* and *rightbound* values are any two constant expressions. It is not necessary for the left bound to be greater than the right bound and either of the bounds is not restricted to be a 0. Here is an example.

> **wire** [3:0] *Out, InA, InB;*
> . . .
> **nand** *Gang* [3 : 0] *(Out, InA, InB);*

This instantiation with the range specification is same as:

> **nand**
>   *Gang3 (Out[3], InA[3], InB[3]),*
>   *Gang2 (Out[2], InA[2], InB[2]),*
>   *Gang1 (Out[1], InA[1], InB[1]),*
>   *Gang0 (Out[0], InA[0], InB[0]);*

Note that the instance name is not optional when specifying an array of instances.

5.10   Implicit Nets

If a net is not declared in a Verilog HDL model, by default, it is implicitly declared as a 1-bit wire. However the `**default_nettype** compiler directive can be used to override the default net type. This compiler directive is of the form:

> `**default_nettype** *net_type*

Here is an example.

```
`default_nettype wand
```

With this directive, all subsequent undeclared nets are of type **wand**.

The `**default_nettype** compiler directive occurs outside of a module definition and stays in effect until the next same directive is reached or a `**resetall** directive is found.

5.11   A Simple Example

Here is a gate-level description of a 4-to-1 multiplexer circuit shown in Figure 5-7. Note that no instance names are specified in the gate instantiations as these are optional (except when used in an array of instances).

```
module MUX4x1 (Z, D0, D1, D2, D3, S0, S1);
  output Z;
  input D0, D1, D2, D3, S0, S1;

  and (T0, D0, S0bar, S1bar),
      (T1, D1, S0bar, S1),
      (T2, D2, S0, S1bar),
      (T3, D3, S0, S1);

  not (S0bar, S0),
      (S1bar, S1);

  or (Z, T0, T1, T2, T3);
endmodule
```

What if the instantiation for the **or** gate was replaced by the following instantiation?

```
or Z (Z, T0, T1, T2, T3);    // Not legal Verilog HDL.
```

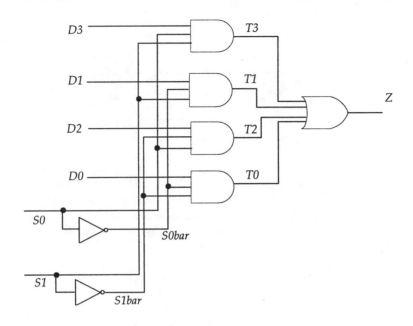

Figure 5-7   A 4-to-1 multiplexer.

Notice that the instance name is also Z and the net connected to the output of the gate is also Z. This is not allowed in Verilog HDL. An instance name cannot be the same as a net name within one module.

5.12   A 2-to-4 Decoder Example

Here is a gate-level description of a 2-to-4 decoder circuit shown in Figure 5-8.

```
module DEC2x4 (A, B, Enable, Z);
  input A, B, Enable;
  output [0:3] Z;
  wire Abar, Bbar;

  not # (1, 2)
    V0 (Abar, A),
```

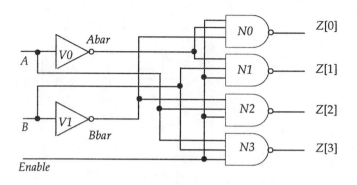

Figure 5-8   A 2-to-4 decoder circuit.

```
V1 (Bbar, B);

nand #(4, 3)
   N0 (Z[0], Enable, Abar, Bbar),
   N1 (Z[1], Enable, Abar, B),
   N2 (Z[2], Enable, A, Bbar),
   N3 (Z[3], Enable, A, B);
endmodule
```

5.13   A Master-slave Flip-flop Example

Here is a gate-level description of a master-slave D-type flip-flop shown in Figure 5-9.

```
module MSDFF (D, C, Q, Qbar);
   input D, C;
   output Q, Qbar;

   not
      NT1 (NotD, D),
      NT2 (NotC, C),
      NT3 (NotY, Y);
```

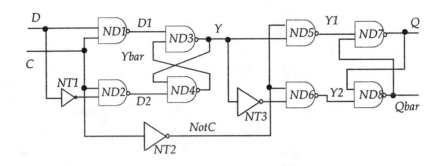

Figure 5-9   A master-slave flip-flop.

```
nand
  ND1 (D1, D, C),
  ND2 (D2, C, NotD),
  ND3 (Y, D1, Ybar),
  ND4 (Ybar, Y, D2),
  ND5 (Y1, Y, NotC),
  ND6 (Y2, NotY, NotC),
  ND7 (Q, Qbar, Y1),
  ND8 (Qbar, Y2, Q);
endmodule
```

5.14   A Parity Circuit

A gate-level model for a 9-bit parity generator, shown in Figure 5-10, is described next.

```
module Parity_9_Bit (D, Even, Odd);
  input [0:8] D;
  output Even, Odd;

  xor #(5, 4)
    XE0 (E0, D[0], D[1]),
    XE1 (E1, D[2], D[3]),
    XE2 (E2, D[4], D[5]),
    XE3 (E3, D[6], D[7]),
    XF0 (F0, E0, E1),
```

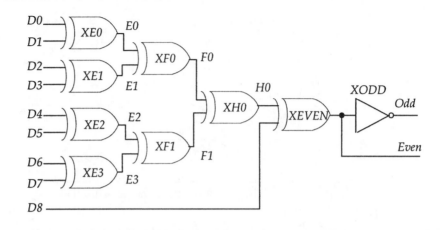

Figure 5-10   A parity generator.

```
      XF1 (F1, E2, E3),
      XH0 (H0, F0, F1),
      XEVEN (Even, D[8], H0);

   not #2
      XODD (Odd, Even);
endmodule
```

5.15   Exercises

1. Model the circuit shown in Figure 5-11 using primitive gates. Write a test bench to test out the circuit. Exercise the circuit with all possible values of inputs.

2. Model the circuit of a priority encoder shown in Figure 5-12 using primitive gates. Output *Valid* is 0 when all inputs are 0, otherwise it is a 1. Write a test bench and verify that the model behaves as a priority encoder.

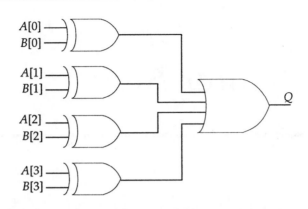

Figure 5-11   Logic for *A* not equals *B*.

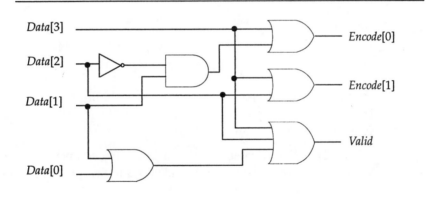

Figure 5-12   Priority encoder.

❑

Chapter 6

USER-DEFINED PRIMITIVES

In the previous chapter, we looked at the built-in primitive gates provided by Verilog HDL. This chapter describes the Verilog HDL capability of specifying user-defined primitives (UDP).

A UDP is instantiated exactly the same way as a primitive gate, that is, the syntax for an UDP instantiation is identical to that of a gate instantiation.

6.1   Defining a UDP

A UDP is defined using a UDP declaration which has the following syntax.

```
primitive UDP_name ( OutputName , List_of_inputs );
    Output_declaration
    List_of_input_declarations
    [ Reg_declaration ]
    [ Initial_statement ]
```

```
table
  List_of_table_entries
endtable
endprimitive
```

A UDP definition does not depend on a module definition and thus appears outside of a module definition. A UDP definition can also be in a separate text file.

A UDP can have only one output and may have one or more inputs. The first port must be the output port. In addition, the output can have the value 0, 1 or x (z is not allowed). If a value z appears on the input, it is treated as an x. The behavior of a UDP is described in the form of a table.

The following two kinds of behavior can be described in an UDP.

i.   Combinational.

ii.   Sequential (edge-triggered and level-sensitive).

6.2   Combinational UDP

In a combinational UDP, the table specifies the various input combinations and their corresponding output values. Any combination that is not specified is an x for the output. Here is an example of a 2-to-1 multiplexer.

```
primitive MUX2x1 (Z, Hab, Bay, Sel);
  output Z;
  input Hab, Bay, Sel;

  table
  //Hab  Bay  Sel  : Z   Note: This line is only a comment.
     0    ?    1    : 0 ;
     1    ?    1    : 1 ;
     ?    0    0    : 0 ;
     ?    1    0    : 1 ;
     0    0    x    : 0 ;
     1    1    x    : 1 ;
  endtable
endprimitive
```

The ? character represents a don't-care value, that is, it could either be a 0, 1 or x. The order of the input ports must match the order of entries in the table, that is, the first column in the table corresponds to the first input in the module port list (which is *Hab*), second column is *Bay* and the third column is *Sel*. In the table for the multiplexer, there is no table entry for one input combination **01x** (there are others as well); in this case, the output defaults to an x (as also for other unspecified entries).

Here is an example of a 4-to-1 multiplexer, shown in Figure 6-1, formed using 2-to-1 multiplexer primitives.

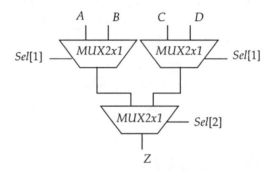

Figure 6-1 A 4-to-1 multiplexer built using UDPs.

```
module MUX4x1 (Z, A, B, C, D, Sel);
    input A, B, C, D;
    input [2:1] Sel;
    output Z;
    parameter tRISE = 2, tFALL = 3;

    MUX2x1 #(tRISE, tFALL)
        (TL, A, B, Sel[1]),
        (TP, C, D, Sel[1]),
        (Z, TL, TP, Sel[2]);
endmodule
```

In case of a UDP instantiation, up to two delays can be specified as shown in the above example. This is because the output of an UDP can either get a value 0 or a value 1, or the value x (there is no turn-off delay).

6.3   Sequential UDP

In a sequential UDP, the internal state is described using a 1-bit register. The value of this register is the output of the sequential UDP.

There are two different kinds of sequential UDP, one that models level-sensitive behavior and another that models edge-sensitive behavior.

A sequential UDP uses the current value of the register and the input values to determine the next value of the register (and consequently the output).

6.3.1   Initializing the State Register

The state of a sequential UDP can be initialized by using an initial statement that has one procedural assignment statement. This is of the form:

```
initial reg_name = 0, 1 or x;
```

This initial statement appears within the UDP definition.

6.3.2   Level-sensitive Sequential UDP

Here is an example of a level-sensitive sequential UDP that models a D-type latch. As long as the clock is 0, data passes from the input to the output, else the value remains latched.

```
primitive Latch (Q, Clk, D);
  output Q;
  reg Q;
  input Clk, D;

  table
  // Clk   D     Q (state)  Q(next)
       0    1    : ?       :   1 ;
       0    0    : ?       :   0 ;
       1    ?    : ?       :   - ;
  endtable
endprimitive
```

93

The − character implies a "no change". Note that the state of the UDP is stored in register Q.

6.3.3   Edge-triggered Sequential UDP

Here is an example of a D-type edge-triggered flip-flop modeled as a edge-triggered sequential UDP. An initial statement is used to initialize the state of the flip-flop.

```
primitive D_Edge_FF (Q, Clk, Data);
  output Q;
  reg Q;
  input Data, Clk;

  initial Q = 0;

  table
    // Clk   Data     Q (state)   Q(next)
       (01)    0   :     ?     :   0 ;
       (01)    1   :     ?     :   1 ;
       (0x)    1   :     1     :   1 ;
       (0x)    0   :     0     :   0 ;
       // Ignore negative edge of clock:
       (?0)    ?   :     ?     :   − ;
       // Ignore data changes on steady clock:
       ?     (??):     ?     :   − ;
  endtable
endprimitive
```

The table entry (01) indicates a transition from 0 to 1, the entry (0x) indicates a transition from 0 to x, the entry (?0) indicates a transition from any value (0, 1, or x) to 0, and the entry (??) indicates any transition. For any unspecified transition, the output defaults to an x.

Given the UDP definition of the *D_Edge_FF*, it can now be instantiated in a module just like a primitive gate as shown in the following example of a 4-bit register.

```
module Reg4 (Clk, Din, Dout);
  input Clk;
  input [0:3] Din;
  output [0:3] Dout;

  D_Edge_FF
        DLAB0 (Dout[0], Clk, Din[0]),
        DLAB1 (Dout[1], Clk, Din[1]),
        DLAB2 (Dout[2], Clk, Din[2]),
        DLAB3 (Dout[3], Clk, Din[3]);
endmodule
```

6.3.4   Mixing Edge-triggered and Level-sensitive Behavior

It is possible to mix level-sensitive entries and edge-triggered entries in one table. In such a case, the edge transitions are processed before the level-sensitive ones are processed, that is, the level-sensitive entries override the edge-triggered entries.

Here is an example of a D-type flip-flop with an asynchronous clear.

```
primitive D_Async_FF (Q, Clk, Clr, Data);
  output Q;
  reg Q;
  input Clr, Data, Clk;

  table
  // Clk   Clr  Data    Q(state)  Q(next)
      (01)   0    0   :   ?     :   0 ;
      (01)   0    1   :   ?     :   1 ;
      (0x)   0    1   :   1     :   1 ;
      (0x)   0    0   :   0     :   0 ;
      // Ignore negative edge of clock:
      (?0)   0    ?   :   ?     :   - ;
      (??)   1    ?   :   ?     :   0;
      ?      1    ?   :   ?     :   0;
  endtable
endprimitive
```

6.4   Another Example

Here is a UDP description of a 3-bit majority circuit. The output is 1 if the input vector has two or more 1's.

```
primitive Majority3 (Z, A, B, C);
  input A, B, C;
  output Z;

  table
    //A  B  C  :  Z
      0  0  ?  :  0;
      0  ?  0  :  0;
      ?  0  0  :  0;
      1  1  ?  :  1;
      1  ?  1  :  1;
      ?  1  1  :  1;
    endtable
endprimitive
```

6.5   Summary of Table Entries

For sake of completion, listed in the table below are all the possible values that could be used in a table entry.

Symbol	Meaning
0	logic 0
1	logic 1
x	unknown
?	any of 0, 1, or x
b	any of 0 or 1
–	no change
(AB)	value change from A to B

Symbol	Meaning
*	same as (??)
r	same as (01)
f	same as (10)
p	any of (01), (0x), (x1)
n	any of (10), (1x), (x0)

6.6   Exercises

1. How is a combinational UDP different from a sequential UDP?

2. A UDP can have one or more outputs. True or False?

3. Can an initial statement be used to initialize a combinational UDP?

4. Write a UDP description for the priority encoder circuit shown in Figure 5-12. Verify the model using a test bench.

5. Write a UDP description for a toggle-type flip-flop. In a toggle flip-flop, if data input is 0, output does not change. If data input is a 1, then on every clock edge, the output toggles. Assume that the triggering clock edge is a negative clock edge. Verify the model using a test bench.

6. Model a rising-edge triggered JK flip-flop as a UDP. If both inputs, J and K, are 0, output does not change. If J is 0 and K is a 1, then output is 0. If J is 1 and K is 0, then output is 1. If J and K are both 1, output toggles. Verify the model using a test bench.

❏

Chapter 7

DATAFLOW MODELING

This chapter describes the continuous assignment feature of Verilog HDL. Continuous assignments model dataflow behavior; in contrast, procedural assignments (the topic of next chapter) model sequential behavior. Combinational logic behavior can be best modeled using continuous assignments.

7.1   Continuous Assignment

A continuous assignment assigns a value to a net (it cannot be used to assign a value to a register). It has the following form (a simple form):

```
assign LHS_target = RHS_expression ;
```

For example,

```
wire [3:0] Z, Preset, Clear;      // Net declaration.

assign Z = Preset & Clear;        // Continuous assignment.
```

The target of the continuous assignment is Z and the right-hand side expression is "*Preset & Clear*". Note the presence of the keyword **assign** in the continuous assignment.

When does a continuous assignment execute? Whenever an event (an event is a change of value) occurs on an operand used in the right-hand side expression, the expression is evaluated and if the result value is different, it is then assigned to the left-hand side target.

In the above example, if either *Preset* or *Clear* change, the entire right-hand side expression is evaluated. If this results in a change of value, then the resultant value is assigned to the net Z.

The target in a continuous assignment can be one of the following.

    i.   Scalar net

    ii.   Vector net

    iii. Constant bit-select of a vector

    iv. Constant part-select of a vector

    v.   Concatenation of any of the above

Here are more examples of continuous assignments.

```
assign BusErr = Parity | (One & OP);

assign Z = ~ (A | B) & (C | D) & (E | F);
```

The last continuous assignment executes whenever there is a change of value in A, B, C, D, E or F, in which case, the entire right-hand side expression is evaluated and the result is then assigned to the target Z.

In the next example, the target is a concatenation of a scalar net and a vector net.

```
wire Cout, Cin;
wire [3:0] Sum, A, B;
. . .
assign {Cout, Sum} = A + B + Cin;
```

Since A and B are 4-bits wide, the result of addition can produce a maximum of a 5-bit result. The left-hand side is specified to be five bits (one bit for *Cout* and 4 bits of *Sum*). The assignment therefore causes the rightmost four bits of the right-hand side expression result to be assigned to *Sum* and the fifth bit (the carry bit) to *Cout*.

The next example shows how multiple assignments can be written in one continuous statement.

```
assign Mux = (S == 0) ? A : 'bz,
       Mux = (S == 1) ? B : 'bz,
       Mux = (S == 2) ? C : 'bz,
       Mux = (S == 3) ? D : 'bz;
```

This is a short form of writing the following four separate continuous assignments.

```
assign Mux = (S == 0) ? A : 'bz;
assign Mux = (S == 1) ? B : 'bz;
assign Mux = (S == 2) ? C : 'bz;
assign Mux = (S == 3) ? D : 'bz;
```

7.2   An Example

Here is an example of a 1-bit full-adder described using the dataflow style.

```
module FA_Df (A, B, Cin, Sum, Cout);
  input A, B, Cin;
  output Sum, Cout;

  assign Sum = A ^ B ^ Cin;
  assign Cout = (A & Cin) | (B & Cin) | (A & B);
endmodule
```

In this example, there are two continuous assignments. These assignments are concurrent in the sense that they are order independent. These continuous assignments execute based on events that occur on operands used in the right-hand side expression. If *A* changes, both the continuous assignments are evaluated, that is, the right-hand side expressions are evaluated and the results are assigned to the left-hand side targets concurrently.

7.3   Net Declaration Assignment

A continuous assignment can appear as part of a net declaration itself. Such an assignment is called a *net declaration assignment*. Here is an example.

```
wire [3:0] Sum = 4'b0;
wire Clear = 'b1;

wire A_GT_B = A > B, B_GT_A = B > A;
```

A net declaration assignment declares the net along with a continuous assignment. It is a convenient form of declaring a net and then writing a continuous assignment. See the example below.

```
wire Clear;
assign Clear = 'b1;
```

is equivalent to the net declaration assignment:

```
wire Clear = 'b1;
```

Multiple net declaration assignments on the same net are not allowed. If multiple assignments are necessary, continuous assignments must be used.

7.4   Delays

If no delay is specified in a continuous assignment, as in the previous examples, the assignment of the right-hand side expression to the left-hand side target occurs with zero delay. A delay can be explicitly specified in a continuous assignment as shown in the following example.

```
assign #6 Ask = Quiet || Late;
```

The delay specified, #6, is the delay between the right-hand side and the left-hand side. For example, if a change of value occurs on *Late* at time 5, then the expression on the right-hand side of the assignment is evaluated at time 5 and *Ask* will be assigned a new value at time 11 (= 5 + 6). The delay concept is illustrated in Figure 7-1.

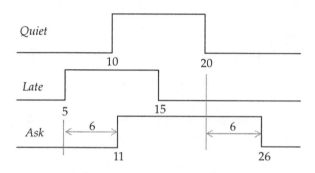

Figure 7-1   Delay in a continuous assignment.

What happens if the right-hand side changes before it had a chance to propagate to the left-hand side? In such a case, the latest value change is applied. Here is an example that shows this behavior.

```
assign #4 Cab = Drm;
```

Figure 7-2 shows the effect. The changes on the right-hand side that occur within the delay interval are filtered out. For example, the rising edge on *Drm* at 5 gets scheduled to appear on *Cab* at 9, however since *Drm* goes back to 0 at 8, the scheduled value on *Cab* is deleted. Similarly, the pulse on *Drm* occurring between 18 and 20 gets filtered out. This corresponds to the inertial delay behavior; that is, a value change on the right-hand side must hold steady for at least the delay period before it can propagate to the left-hand side; if the value on the right-hand side changes within the delay period, the former value does not propagate to the output.

For each delay specification, up to three delay values can be specified.

    i.   Rise delay

    ii. Fall delay

    iii. Turn-off delay

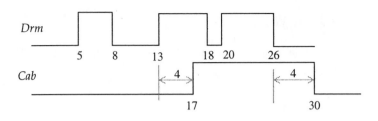

Figure 7-2 Values changing faster than delay interval.

Here is the syntax for specifying the three delays.

        assign #(*rise* , *fall* , *turn-off*) *LHS_target* = *RHS_expression* ;

Here are some examples that show how delays are interpreted when zero to three delay values are specified.

    assign #4 *Ask* = *Quiet* || *Late*;   // One delay value.

    assign #(4, 8) *Ask* = *Quick*;   // Two delay values.

    assign #(4, 8, 6) *Arb* = & *DataBus*;   // Three delay values.

    assign *Bus* = *MemAddr*[7:4];   // No delay value.

In the first assignment statement, the rise delay, the fall delay and the turn-off delay and the transition to **x** delay are the same, which is 4. In the second statement, the rise delay is 4, the fall delay is 8 and the transition to **x** and **z** delay are the same, which is the minimum of 4 and 8, which is 4. In the third assignment, the rise delay is 4, the fall delay is 8 and the turn-off delay is 6; the transition to **x** delay is 4 (the minimum of 4, 8 and 6). In the last statement, all delays are zero.

What does a rise delay mean for a vector net target? If the right-hand side goes from a non-zero value to a zero vector, then fall delay is used. If right-hand side value goes to **z**, then turn-off delay is used; else rise delay is used.

7.5   Net Delays

A delay can also be specified in a net declaration, such as in the following declaration.

wire #5 Arb;

This delay indicates the delay between a change of value of a driver for *Arb* and the net *Arb* itself. Consider the following continuous assignment to the net *Arb*.

assign #2 Arb = Bod & Cap;

An event on *Bod*, say at time 10, causes the right-hand side expression to be evaluated. If the result is different, it is assigned to *Arb* after 2 time units, that is, at time 12. However since *Arb* has a net delay specified, the actual assignment to the net *Arb* occurs at time 17 (= 10 + 2 + 5). The waveforms in Figure 7-3 illustrates the different delays.

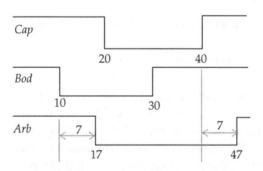

Figure 7-3   Net delay with assignment delay.

The effect of a net delay is best described as shown in Figure 7-4. First the assignment delay is used and then any net delay is added on.

If a delay is present in a net declaration assignment, then the delay is not a net delay but an assignment delay. In the following net declaration assignment for *A*, 2 time units is the assignment delay, not the net delay.

```
wire #2 A = B - C;              // Assignment delay.
```

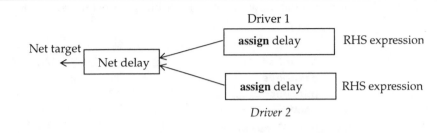

Figure 7-4   Effect of net delay.

7.6   Examples

7.6.1   Master-slave Flip-flop

Here is a Verilog HDL model for the master-slave flip-flop shown in Figure 5-9.

```
module MSDFF_DF (D, C, Q, Qbar);
  input D, C;
  output Q, Qbar;
  wire NotC, NotD, NotY, Y, D1, D2, Ybar, Y1, Y2;

  assign NotD = ~ D;
  assign NotC = ~ C;
  assign NotY = ~ Y;

  assign D1 = ~ (D & C);
  assign D2 = ~ (C & NotD);
  assign Y = ~ (D1 & Ybar);
  assign Ybar = ~ (Y & D2);
  assign Y1 = ~ (Y & NotC);
  assign Y2 = ~ (NotY & NotC);
  assign Q = ~ (Qbar & Y1);
  assign Qbar = ~ (Y2 & Q);
endmodule
```

7.6.2   Magnitude Comparator

Here is a dataflow model for a 8-bit (parameterized) magnitude comparator.

```
module MagnitudeComparator (A, B, AgtB, AeqB, AltB);
  parameter BUS = 8;
  parameter EQ_DELAY = 5, LT_DELAY = 8, GT_DELAY = 8;
  input [1 : BUS] A, B;
  output AgtB, AeqB, AltB;

  assign #EQ_DELAY   AeqB = A == B;
  assign #GT_DELAY   AgtB = A > B;
  assign #LT_DELAY   AltB = A < B;
endmodule
```

7.7   Exercises

1. Give an example of how turn-off delay is used in a continuous assignment.

2. When there are two or more assignments to the same target, how is the effective value for the target determined?

3. Write a dataflow model for the parity generator circuit shown in Figure 5-10. Use only two assignment statements. Specify rise and fall delays as well.

4. Using continuous assignment statements, describe the behavior of the priority encoder circuit shown in Figure 5-12.

5. Given:
    tri0 [4:0] *Qbus*;
    assign *Qbus* = *Sbus*;
    assign *Qbus* = *Pbus*;

    What is the value on *Qbus* if both *Pbus* and *Sbus* are all **z**'s.

□

Chapter 8

BEHAVIORAL MODELING

In previous chapters, we have examined gate-level modeling using gate and UDP instantiations, and dataflow modeling using continuous assignments. This chapter describes the third style of modeling in Verilog HDL, which is, behavioral modeling. To use the full power of Verilog HDL, a model may contain a mix of all the three styles of modeling.

8.1   Procedural Constructs

The primary mechanisms for modeling the behavior of a design are the following two statements.

    i.   Initial statement

    ii. Always statement

A module may contain an arbitrary number of initial or always statements. These statements execute concurrently with respect to each other, that is, the order of these statements in a module is not important. An execution of an initial or an always statement starts a separate control flow. All initial and always statements execute concurrently starting at time 0.

8.1.1   Initial Statement

An initial statement executes only once. It begins its execution at start of simulation which is at time 0. The syntax for the initial statement is:

initial
  [*timing_control*] *procedural_statement*

where a *procedural_statement* is one of:

procedural_assignment (blocking or non-blocking)
procedural_continuous_assignment
conditional_statement
case_statement
loop_statement
wait_statement
disable_statement
event_trigger
sequential_block
parallel_block
task_enable (user or system)

The sequential block (**begin**...**end**) is the most commonly used procedural statement. Here *timing_control* can be a delay control, that is, wait for a certain time, or an event control, that is, wait for an event to occur or a condition to become true. The execution of an initial statement causes the procedural statement to execute once. Note that an initial statement starts execution at time 0. It may complete execution at a later time depending on any timing controls present in the procedural statement.

Here is an example of an initial statement.

reg *Yurt*;
  . . .
initial
  Yurt = 2;

The initial statement contains a procedural assignment with no timing control. The initial statement executes at time 0, which causes *Yurt* to be assigned the value 2 at time 0. Here is another example of an initial statement, this time with a timing control.

```
reg Curt;
  . . .
initial
  #2 Curt = 1;
```

Register *Curt* gets assigned the value 1 at time 2. The initial statement starts execution at time 0 but completes execution at time 2.

Here is an example of an initial statement with a sequential block.

```
parameter SIZE = 1024;
reg [7:0] RAM[0: SIZE-1];
reg RibReg;

initial
  begin: SEQ_BLK_A
    integer Index;

    RibReg = 0;
    for (Index = 0; Index < SIZE; Index = Index + 1)
      RAM[Index] = 0;
  end
```

The sequential block, demarcated by the keywords **begin**...**end**, contains procedural statements that execute sequentially, as in a high-level programming language such as *C. SEQ_BLK_A* is the label for the sequential block; this label is not required if no local declarations are present in the block, for example, if the declaration for *Index* were outside the initial statement, no label would be required. An integer *Index* has been locally declared within this block. Furthermore, the sequential block contains one procedural assignment followed by a for-loop statement. This initial statement, upon execution, initializes all memory locations with value 0.

Here is another example of an initial statement with a sequential block. In this example, the sequential block contains procedural assignments with timing controls.

```
// Waveform generation:
parameter APPLY_DELAY = 5;
reg [0:7] Port_A;
   . . .
initial
  begin
    Port_A = 'h20;
    #APPLY_DELAY Port_A = 'hF2;
    #APPLY_DELAY Port_A = 'h41;
    #APPLY_DELAY Port_A = 'h0A;
  end
```

Upon execution, *Port_A* will get values as shown in Figure 8-1.

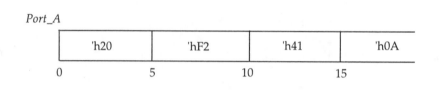

Figure 8-1   A waveform produced using an initial statement.

An initial statement is mainly used for initialization and waveform generation as shown in the examples above.

8.1.2   Always Statement

In contrast to the initial statement, an always statement executes repeatedly. Just like the initial statement, an always statement also begins execution at time 0. The syntax for an always statement is:

```
always
  [ timing_control ] procedural_statement
```

where *procedural_statement* and *timing_control* are as described in the previous section.

Here is an example of an always statement.

```
always
  Clk = ~ Clk;
// Will loop indefinitely.
```

This always statement has one procedural assignment. Since the always statement executes repeatedly and there is no timing control specified, the procedural assignment statement will loop indefinitely in zero time. Therefore, an always statement must always have some sort of timing control.

Here is the same always statement, this time with a delay control.

```
always
  #5 Clk = ~ Clk;
// Waveform on Clk of period 10.
```

This always statement, upon execution, produces a waveform with a period of 10 time units.

Here is an example of an always statement with a sequential block that is controlled by an event control.

```
reg [0:5] InstrReg;
reg [3:0] Accum;
wire ExecuteCycle;

always
  @(ExecuteCycle)
    begin
      case (InstrReg[0:1])
        2'b00 : Store (Accum, InstrReg[2:5]);
        2'b11 : Load (Accum, InstrReg[2:5]);
        2'b01 : Jump (InstrReg[2:5]);
        2'b10 : ;
      endcase
    end
// Store, Load and Jump are user-defined
// tasks defined elsewhere.
```

Statements within a sequential block (**begin**...**end**) execute sequentially with respect to each other. This always statement implies that whenever an event occurs on *ExecuteCycle*, that is, whenever it changes, execute the sequential block; execution of the sequential block implies executing all statements within the block sequentially.

Here is another example. The model is that of a negative edge-triggered D-type flip-flop with an asynchronous preset.

```
module DFF (Clk, D, Set, Q, Qbar);
  input Clk, D, Set;
  output Q, Qbar;
  reg Q, Qbar;

  always
    wait (Set == 1)
      begin
        #3 Q = 1;
        #2 Qbar = 0;
        wait (Set == 0);
      end

  always
    @(negedge Clk)
      begin
        if (Set != 1)
          begin
            #5 Q = D;
            #1 Qbar = ~Q;
          end
      end
endmodule
```

This module has two always statements. The first always statement has a level-sensitive event control with a sequential block. The second always statement has an edge-triggered timing control with a sequential block.

8.1.3   In One Module

A module may contain multiple always statements and multiple initial statements. Each statement starts a separate control flow. Each statement starts execution at time 0.

Here is an example of a module with one initial statement and two always statements.

```
module TestXorBehavior;
  reg Sa, Sb, Zeus;

  initial
    begin
      Sa = 0;
      Sb = 0;
      #5 Sb = 1;
      #5 Sa = 1;
      #5 Sb = 0;
    end

  always
    @(Sa or Sb)  Zeus = Sa ^ Sb;

  always
    @(Zeus)
      $display ("At time %t, Sa = %d, Sb = %d, Zeus = %b",
                $time, Sa, Sb, Zeus);
endmodule
```

The order of the three statements in the module is not important since they all execute concurrently. The initial statement when executed causes the first statement in the sequential block to execute, that is, Sa gets assigned 0; the next statement executes immediately after zero delay. The #5 in the third line of the initial statement indicates a "wait for 5 time units". Thus Sb gets a 1 after 5 time units, Sa gets a 1 after another 5 time units and finally Sb gets a 0 after another 5 time units. After the last statement in the sequential block is executed, the initial statement suspends forever.

The first always statement waits for an event to occur on Sa or Sb. Whenever such an event occurs, the statement within the always statement is executed and then the always statement again waits for an event to occur on Sa or Sb. Notice that based on the values assigned to Sa and Sb in the initial statement, the always statement will be executed at times 0, 5, 10 and 15 time units.

Similarly the second always statement executes whenever an event occurs on $Zeus$. In such a case, the $display system task is executed and then the always statement again waits for an event to occur on $Zeus$. Figure 8-2 shows the waveforms produced on Sa, Sb and $Zeus$. Here is the output produced when the module is simulated.

113

At time   5, Sa = 0, Sb = 1, Zeus = 1
At time   10, Sa = 1, Sb = 1, Zeus = 0
At time   15, Sa = 1, Sb = 0, Zeus = 1

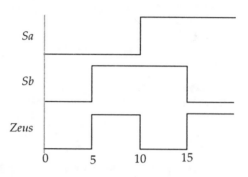

Figure 8-2   Waveforms produced on *Sa*, *Sb* and *Zeus*.

8.2   Timing Controls

A timing control may be associated with a procedural statement. Timing control is of two forms:

i.   Delay control.

ii.   Event control.

8.2.1   Delay Control

A delay control is of the form:

```
#delay  procedural_statement
```

as in the example:

```
#2    Tx = Rx - 5;
```

A delay control specifies the time duration from the time the statement is initially encountered to the time the statement executes. Basically it means "wait for delay" before executing the statement. In the above example, the procedural assignment statement is executed two time units after the statement is reached; it is equivalent to wait for 2 time units and then execute the assignment.

Here is another example.

```
initial
  begin
    #3 Wave = 'b0111;
    #6 Wave = 'b1100;
    #7 Wave = 'b0000;
  end
```

The initial statement executes at time 0. First, wait for 3 time units, execute the first assignment, wait for another 6 time units, execute the second statement, wait for 7 more time units, execute the third statement and then suspend indefinitely.

A delay control can also be specified in the form:

```
#delay ;
```

This statement causes a wait for the specified delay before the next statement is executed. Here is an example of such an usage.

```
parameter ON_DELAY = 3, OFF_DELAY = 5;
always
  begin
    # ON_DELAY;          // wait for ON_DELAY.
    RefClk = 0;
    # OFF_DELAY;         // wait for OFF_DELAY.
    RefClk = 1;
  end
```

The delay in a delay control can be an arbitrary expression, that is, it need not be restricted to a constant. See the following examples.

```
#Strobe
  Compare = Tx ^ Mask;

#(PERIOD / 2)
  Clock = ~ Clock;
```

If the value of the delay expression is 0, then it is called an *explicit zero delay*.

```
#0;             // Explicit zero delay.
```

An explicit zero delay causes a wait until all other events that are waiting to be executed at the current simulation time are completed, before it resumes; the simulation time does not advance.

If the value of a delay expression is an x or a z, it is the same as zero delay. If the delay expression evaluates to a negative value, the two's complement signed integer value is used as the delay.

8.2.2   Event Control

With an event control, a statement executes based on events. There are two kinds of event control.

    i.   Edge-triggered event control

    ii. Level-sensitive event control

Edge-triggered Event Control

An edge-triggered event control is of the form:

```
@ event  procedural_statement
```

as in the example:

```
@ (posedge Clock)
  Curr_State = Next_State;
```

An event control with a procedural statement delays the execution of the statement until the occurrence of the specified event. In the above example, if a positive edge occurs on *Clock* the assignment statement executes, otherwise execution is suspended until a positive edge occurs on *Clock*.

Here are some more examples.

```
@ (negedge Reset)    Count = 0;


@Cla
  Zoo = Foo;
```

In the first statement, the assignment statement executes only when a negative edge occurs on *Reset*. In the second statement, *Foo* is assigned to *Zoo* when an event occurs on *Cla*, that is, wait for an event to occur on *Cla*, when it does occur, assign *Foo* to *Zoo*.

Event control can also be of the form:

```
@ event ;
```

This statement causes a wait until the specified event occurs. Here is an example of such an usage in an initial statement that determines the on-period of a clock.

```
time RiseEdge, OnDelay;

initial
  begin
    // Wait until positive edge on clock occurs:
    @ (posedge ClockA);
    RiseEdge = $time;
    // Wait until negative edge on clock occurs:
    @ (negedge ClockA);
    OnDelay = $time - RiseEdge;
    $display ("The on-period of clock is %t.", OnDelay);
  end
```

Events can also be or'ed to indicate "if any of the events occur". This is shown in the following examples.

```
@ (posedge Clear or negedge Reset)
   Q = 0;

@ (Ctrl_A or Ctrl_B)
   Dbus = 'bz;
```

Note that the keyword **or** does not imply a logical-or such as in an expression.

posedge and **negedge** are keywords in Verilog HDL that indicate a positive edge and a negative edge respectively. A negative edge is one of the following transitions:

```
1 -> x
1 -> z
1 -> 0
x -> 0
z -> 0
```

A positive edge is one of the following transitions:

```
0 -> x
0 -> z
0 -> 1
x -> 1
z -> 1
```

Level-sensitive Event Control

In a level-sensitive event control, the procedural statement is delayed until a condition becomes true. This event control is written in the form:

```
wait (condition)
   procedural_statement
```

The procedural statement executes only if the condition is true, else it waits until the condition becomes true. If the condition is already true when the statement is reached, then the procedural statement is executed immediately. The procedural statement is optional.

Here are some examples.

```
wait (Sum > 22)
  Sum = 0;

wait (DataReady)
  Data = Bus;

wait (Preset);
```

In the first statement, only when *Sum* becomes greater than 22 will the assignment of 0 to *Sum* occur. In the second example, *Bus* is assigned to *Data* only if *DataReady* is true, that is, *DataReady* has the value 1. In the last example, the execution is simply delayed until *Preset* becomes true.

8.3   Block Statement

A block statement provides a mechanism to group two or more statements to act syntactically like a single statement. There are two kinds of blocks in Verilog HDL. These are:

i.   Sequential block (**begin**...**end**): Statements are executed sequentially in the given order.

ii. Parallel block (**fork**...**join**): Statements in this block execute concurrently.

A block can be labeled optionally. If so labeled, registers can be declared locally within the block. Blocks can also be referenced; for example, a block can be disabled using a disable statement. A block label, in addition, provides a way to uniquely identify registers. However, there is one word of caution. All local registers are static, that is, their values remain valid throughout the entire simulation run.

8.3.1   Sequential Block

Statements in a sequential block execute in sequence. A delay value in each statement is relative to the simulation time of the execution of the previous statement. Once a sequential block completes execution, execution continues with the next statement following the sequential block. Here is the syntax of a sequential block.

```
begin
  [ : block_id { declarations } ]
  procedural_statement (s)
end
```

Here is an example of a sequential block.

```
// Waveform generation:
begin
  #2 Stream = 1;
  #5 Stream = 0;
  #3 Stream = 1;
  #4 Stream = 0;
  #2 Stream = 1;
  #5 Stream = 0;
end
```

Assume that the sequential block gets executed at 10 time units. The first statement executes after 2 time units, that is at 12 time units. After this execution has completed, the next statement is executed at 17 time units (because of the delay). Then the next statement is executed at 20 time units and so on. Figure 8-3 shows the waveform produced due to the sequential execution behavior of this example.

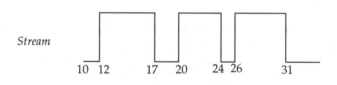

Figure 8-3   Delays are cumulative in a sequential block.

Here is another example of a sequential block.

```
begin
  Pat = Mask | Mat;
  @ (negedge Clk)
    FF = & Pat;
end
```

In this example, the first statement executes first and then the second statement executes. Of course, the assignment in the second statement occurs only when a negative edge appears on *Clk*. Here is another example of a sequential block.

```
begin: SEQ_BLK
  reg [0:3] Sat;

  Sat = Mask & Data;
  FF = ^ Sat;
end
```

In this example, the sequential block has a label *SEQ_BLK* and it has a local register declared. Upon execution, the first statement is executed, then the second statement is executed.

8.3.2   Parallel Block

A parallel block has the delimiters **fork** and **join** (a sequential block has the delimiters **begin** and **end**). Statements in a parallel block execute concurrently. Delay values specified in each statement within a parallel block are relative to the time the block starts its execution. When the last activity in the parallel block has completed execution (this need not be the last statement), execution continues after the block statement. Stated another way, all statements within the parallel block must complete execution before control passes out of the block. Here is the syntax of a parallel block.

```
fork
  [ : block_id { declarations } ]
  procedural_statement (s)
join
```

Here is an example.

```
// Waveform generation:
fork
  #2 Stream = 1;
  #7 Stream = 0;
  #10 Stream = 1;
  #14 Stream = 0;
```

```
    #16 Stream = 1;
    #21 Stream = 0;
join
```

If the parallel block gets executed at 10 time units, all statements execute concurrently and all delay values are relative to 10. For example, the third assignment executes at 20 time units, the fifth assignment executes at 26 time units, and so on. Figure 8-4 shows the waveform produced.

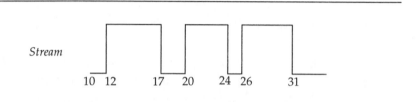

Figure 8-4   Delays are relative in a parallel block.

Here is an example that uses a mix of sequential and parallel blocks to emphasize their differences.

```
always
  begin: SEQ_A
    #4 Dry = 5;              // S1

    fork: PAR_A              // S2
      #6 Cun = 7;            // P1

      begin: SEQ_B           // P2
        Exe = Box;           // S6
        #5 Jap = Exe;        // S7
      end

      #2 Dop = 3;            // P3
      #4 Gos = 2;            // P4
      #8 Pas = 4;            // P5
    join

    #8 Bax = 1;              // S3
    #2 Zoom = 52;            // S4
    #6 $stop;                // S5
  end
```

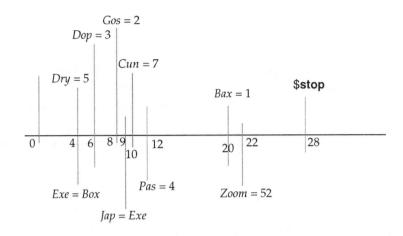

Figure 8-5   Delays due to a mix of sequential and parallel blocks.

The always statement contains a sequential block *SEQ_A* and all statements within the sequential block (S1, S2, S3, S4, S5) execute sequentially. Since the always statement executes at time 0, *Dry* gets assigned 5 at 4 time units, and the parallel block *PAR_A* begins its execution at 4 time units. All statements within the parallel block (P1, P2, P3, P4, P5) execute concurrently, that is, at 4 time units. Thus *Cun* gets assigned a value at 10 time units, *Dop* gets assigned at 6, *Gos* gets assigned at 8, and *Pas* gets assigned at 12. The sequential block *SEQ_B* starts execution at 4 time units, causing statements S6 and then S7 to execute. *Jap* gets its new value at 9. Since all statements within the parallel block *PAR_A* complete execution at time 12, statement S3 is executed at 12 time units, assignment to *Bax* occurs at 20, then statement S4 executes, assignment to *Zoom* occurs at 22, then the next statement executes. Finally the system task $**stop** executes at time 28. Figure 8-5 shows the events that occur upon the execution of the always statement.

8.4   Procedural Assignments

A procedural assignment is an assignment within an initial statement or an always statement. It is used to assign to only a register data type. The right-hand side of the assignment can be any expression. Here is an example.

```
reg [1:4] Enable, A, B;
. . .
#5 Enable = ~ A & ~ B;
```

Enable is a register. Due to the delay control, the assignment statement executes 5 time units after the statement is initially encountered. The right-hand side expression is then evaluated and its value is assigned to *Enable*.

A procedural assignment executes sequentially with respect to other statements that appear around it. Here is an example of an always statement.

```
always
  @ (A or B or C or D)
    begin: AOI
      reg Temp1, Temp2;

      Temp1 = A & B;
      Temp2 = C & D;
      Temp1 = Temp1 | Temp2;
      Z = ~ Temp1;
    end
  /* It is possible to replace the above four statements with
     one statement, such as:
         Z = ~ ((A & B) | (C & D));
     However, it has been used here as such to illustrate the
     sequential nature of the statements in a sequential
     block */
```

The sequential block within the always statement starts execution when an event occurs on *A*, *B*, *C* or *D*. The assignment to *Temp1* takes place first. Then the second assignment occurs. The values of *Temp1* and *Temp2* computed in the previous assignment are used in the third assignment statement. The last assignment uses the value of *Temp1* computed in the third statement.

There are two kinds of procedural assignments.

    i.   Blocking.

    ii. Non-blocking.

But before we discuss these, let us first briefly discuss the notion of intra-statement delays.

8.4.1 Intra-statement Delay

A delay appearing on the left of an expression in an assignment statement is an intra-statement delay. It is the delay by which the right-hand side value is delayed before it is applied to the left-hand side target. Here is an example.

```
Done = #5 'b1;
```

The important thing to note about this delay is that the right-hand side expression is evaluated before the delay, then the wait occurs and then the value is assigned to the left-hand side target. To understand the difference between inter-statement delays and intra-statement delays, here are some examples that illustrate this.

```
Done = #5 'b1;              // Intra-statement delay control.

// is the same as:
begin
  Temp = 'b1;
  #5 Done = Temp;           // Inter-statement delay control.
end

Q = @(posedge Clk) D;      // Intra-statement event control.

// is the same as:
begin
  Temp = D;
  @(posedge Clk)           // Inter-statement event control.
    Q = Temp;
end
```

In addition to the two forms of timing controls (delay control and event control) that can be specified for intra-statement delay, there is yet another form called the repeat event control that can be used to specify intra-statement delay. It is of the form:

```
repeat ( expression ) @ ( event_expression )
```

This form of control is used to specify a delay that is based on the number of occurrences of one or more events. Here is an example.

```
Done = repeat (2) @ (negedge ClkA) A_Reg + B_Reg;
```

This statement when executed evaluates the value of the right-hand side, that is, *A_Reg + B_Reg*, waits for two negative edges on clock *ClkA* and then assigns the value of the right-hand side to *Done*. The equivalent form of this repeat event control example is shown next.

```
begin
  Temp = A_Reg + B_Reg;
  @ (negedge ClkA);
  @ (negedge ClkA);
  Done = Temp;
end
```

This form of delay is useful in synchronizing assignments to certain edges or with a count of edges.

8.4.2   Blocking Procedural Assignment

A procedural assignment in which the assignment operator is an "=" is a blocking procedural assignment. For example,

```
RegA = 52;
```

is a blocking procedural assignment. A blocking procedural assignment is executed before any of the statements that follow it are executed, that is, the assignment statement is executed completely before the next statement is executed. Here is another example.

```
always
  @(A or B or Cin)
    begin: CARRY_OUT
      reg T1, T2, T3;

      T1 = A & B;
      T2 = B & Cin;
      T3 = A & Cin;
      Cout = T1 | T2 | T3;
    end
```

The *T1* assignment occurs first, *T1* is computed, then the second statement executes, *T2* is assigned and then the third statement is executed and *T3* is assigned, and so on.

Here is another example of a blocking procedural assignment using intra-statement delays.

```
initial
  begin
    Clr = #5 0;
    Clr = #4 1;
    Clr = #10 0;
  end
```

The first statement executes at time 0 and *Clr* gets assigned 0 after 5 time units, then the second statement executes causing *Clr* to get assigned a 1 after 4 time units (9 time units from time 0), and then the third statement executes causing *Clr* to get a 0 after 10 time units (19 time units from time 0). The waveform produced on *Clr* is shown in Figure 8-6.

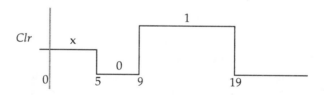

Figure 8-6 Blocking procedural assignments with intra-statement delays.

Here is another example.

```
begin
  Art = 0;
  Art = 1;
end
```

In this case, *Art* gets assigned the value 1. This is because, first *Art* gets assigned 0, then the next statement executes that causes *Art* to get 1 after zero delay. Therefore the assignment of 0 to *Art* is lost.

8.4.3   Non-blocking Procedural Assignment

In a non-blocking procedural assignment, the assignment symbol "<=" is used. Here are some examples of non-blocking procedural assignments.

```
begin
  Load <= 32;
  RegA <= Load;
  RegB <= Store;
end
```

In a non-blocking procedural assignment, the assignment to the target is not blocked (due to delays) but are scheduled to occur in the future (based on the delays; if zero delay, then at the end of the current time step). When a non-blocking procedural assignment is executed, the right-hand side expression is evaluated and its value is scheduled to be assigned to the left-hand side target, and execution continues with the next statement. The earliest an output would be scheduled is at the end of the current time step; this case would occur if there were no delay in the assignment statement. At the end of the current time step or whenever the outputs are scheduled, the assignment to the left-hand side target occurs.

In the above example, let us assume that the sequential block executes at time 10. The first statement causes the value 32 to be assigned to *Load* at the end of time 10, then the second statement executes, the old value of *Load* is used (note that time has not advanced and *Load* in the first assignment has not yet been assigned a new value); the assignment to *RegA* is scheduled at the end of time step 10, the next statement executes and *RegB* is scheduled to be assigned a value at the end of time 10. After all events at time 10 have occurred, all scheduled assignments to the left-hand side target are made.

Here is another example that explains this further.

```
initial
  begin
    Clr <= #5 1;
    Clr <= #4 0;
    Clr <= #10 0;
  end
```

The execution of the first statement causes a 1 to be scheduled to appear on *Clr* at 5 time units, the execution of the second statement causes *Clr* to get a value 0 at 4 time units (4 time units from time 0), and finally the execution of the third statement causes a 0 to be scheduled on *Clr* at 10 time units (10 time units from 0). Note that all the three statements execute at time 0. In addition, notice that the order of execution of non-blocking assignments become irrelevant in this case. Figure 8-7 shows the waveform produced on *Clr*.

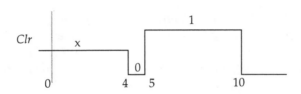

Figure 8-7 Non-blocking assignments with intra-statement delays.

Here is another example, but this time with zero delays.

```
initial
  begin
    Cbn <= 0;
    Cbn <= 1;
  end
```

The value of *Cbn* after the initial statement executes is 1 since the Verilog HDL standard specifies that all non-blocking assignments to a variable shall occur in the order the assignment statements are executed. Thus, *Cbn* gets the value 0 first and then 1.

Here is an example that uses both blocking and non-blocking assignments and highlights their differences.

```
reg [0:2] Q_State;

initial
  begin
    Q_State = 3'b011;
    Q_State <= 3'b100;
```

129

```
                $display ("Current value of Q_State is %b", Q_State);
                #5; // Wait for some time.
                $display ("The delayed value of Q_State is %b",
                          Q_State);
        end
```

The execution of the initial statement produces the result:

Current value of Q_State is 011
The delayed value of Q_State is 100

The first blocking assignment causes *Q_State* to get the value of 3'b011. The execution of the second assignment statement, which is a non-blocking one, causes the value 3'b100 to be scheduled for *Q_State* at the end of the current time step (which is 0). Therefore when the first **$display** task is executed, *Q_State* still has the value from the first assignment, which is 3'b011. When the #5 delay is executed, this causes the scheduled assignment of *Q_State* to occur, *Q_State* gets updated with its new value, a delay of 5 time units occurs and then the next **$display** task is executed, this time displaying the updated value of *Q_State*.

8.4.4   Continuous Assignment vs Procedural Assignment

What are the differences between continuous assignments and procedural assignments? Table 8-1 illustrates this.

Table 8-1   Difference between procedural and continuous assignment.

Procedural assignment	Continuous assignment
Occurs inside an always statement or an initial statement.	Occurs within a module.
Execution is with respect to other statements surrounding it.	Executes concurrently with other statements; executes whenever there is a change of value in an operand on its right-hand side.
Drives registers.	Drives nets.
Uses "=" or "<=" assignment symbol.	Uses "=" assignment symbol.
No **assign** keyword (except in a procedural continuous assignment; see Sec. 8.8).	Uses **assign** keyword.

Here is an example explaining this difference further.

```
module Procedural;
  reg A, B, Z;

  always
    @(B) begin
      Z = A;
      A = B;
    end
endmodule


module Continuous;
  wire A, B, Z;

  assign Z = A;
  assign A = B;
endmodule
```

Say that *B* has an event at time 10ns. In module *Procedural*, the two procedural statements are executed sequentially and *A* gets the new value of *B* at 10ns. *Z* does not get the value of *B* since the assignment to *Z* occurs before the assignment to *A*. In module *Continuous*, the second continuous assignment is triggered since there is an event on *B*. This in turn causes an event on *A*, which causes the first continuous assignment to be executed, which in turn causes *Z* to get the value of *A* which is really *B*. However, if an event occurred on *A*, the always statement in module *Procedural* does not execute since *A* is not in the timing control event list for that always statement. However the first continuous assignment in the module *Continuous* executes and *Z* gets the new value of *A*.

8.5   Conditional Statement

The syntax of an if statement is:

```
if ( condition_1 )
  procedural_statement_1
{ else if ( condition_2 )
```

```
        procedural_statement_2 }
    [ else
        procedural_statement_3 ]
```

If *condition_1* evaluates to a non-zero known value, then the *procedural_statement_1* is executed. If *condition_1* evaluates to a value 0, x or z, the *procedural_statement_1* is not executed, and an else branch, if it exists, is executed. Here is an example.

```
if (Sum < 60)
  begin
    Grade = C;
    Total_C = Total_C + 1;
  end
else if (Sum < 75)
  begin
    Grade = B;
    Total_B = Total_B + 1;
  end
else
  begin
    Grade = A;
    Total_A = Total_A + 1;
  end
```

Note that the condition expression must always be within parenthesis. Also there is a possibility for an ambiguity if an if-if-else form is used, as shown in this example.

```
if (Clk)
  if (Reset)
    Q = 0;
  else
    Q = D;
```

The question is to which if does the last else belong? Does it belong to the first if condition (*Clk*) or to the second if condition (*Reset*)? This is resolved in Verilog HDL by associating the else with the closest if that does not have an else. In this example, the else is associated with the inner if statement.

Here are some more examples of if statements.

```
if (Sum < 100)
  Sum = Sum + 10;


if (Nickel_In)
  Deposit = 5;
else if (Dime_In)
  Deposit = 10;
else if (Quarter_In)
  Deposit = 25;
else
  Deposit = ERROR;


if (Ctrl)
  begin
    if (~Ctrl2)
      Mux = 4'd2;
    else
      Mux = 4'd1;
  end
else
  begin
    if (~Ctrl2)
      Mux = 4'd8;
    else
      Mux = 4'd4;
  end
```

8.6   Case Statement

A case statement is a multi-way conditional branch. It has the following syntax:

```
case ( case_expr )
  case_item_expr {, case_item_expr } : procedural_statement
  . . .
  . . .
```

```
    [ default: procedural_statement ]
endcase
```

The case expression is evaluated first. Next the case item expressions are evaluated and compared in the order given. The set of statements that match the first true condition is executed. Multiple case item expressions can be specified in one branch; these values need not be mutually-exclusive. The default case covers all values that are not covered by the case item expressions.

Neither the case expression nor the case item expressions need be constant expressions. In a case statement, the x and z values are compared as their literal values. Here is an example of a case statement.

```
parameter
    MON = 0, TUE = 1, WED = 2,
    THU = 3, FRI = 4,
    SAT = 5, SUN = 6;
reg [0:2] Day;
integer Pocket_Money;

case (Day)
   TUE    : Pocket_Money = 6;    // Branch 1
   MON,
   WED    : Pocket_Money = 2;    // Branch 2
   FRI,
   SAT,
   SUN    : Pocket_Money = 7;    // Branch 3
   default : Pocket_Money = 0;    // Branch 4
endcase
```

Branch 2 is chosen if *Day* has the value *MON* or *WED*. Branch 3 covers the values *FRI*, *SAT*, *SUN*, while branch 4 covers the remaining values, *THU* and the bit-vector 111. Here is another example of a case statement.

```
module ALU (A, B, OpCode, Z);
   input [3:0] A, B;
   input [1:2] OpCode;
   output [7:0] Z;
   reg [7:0] Z;
```

```
parameter
    ADD_INSTR = 2'b10,
    SUB_INSTR = 2'b11,
    MULT_INSTR = 2'b01,
    DIV_INSTR = 2'b00;

always
  @ (A or B or OpCode)
    case (OpCode)
    ADD_INSTR:      Z = A + B;
    SUB_INSTR:      Z = A - B;
    MULT_INSTR:     Z = A * B;
    DIV_INSTR:      Z = A / B;
    endcase
endmodule
```

What happens if the case expression and the case item expressions are of different lengths? In such a situation, all case expressions are made equal to the largest size of any of these expressions before any comparisons are made. Here is an example that illustrates this.

```
case (3'b101 << 2)
  3'b100   : $display ("First branch taken!");
  4'b0100  : $display ("Second branch taken!");
  5'b10100 : $display ("Third branch taken!");
  default  : $display ("Default branch taken!");
endcase
```

produces:

Third branch taken!

Since the third case item expression is of size 5 bits, all case item expressions and the case expression are made equal to size 5. So when 3'b101 << 2 is computed, the result is 5'b10100, and the third branch is taken.

8.6.1   Don't-cares in Case

In the case statement described in the previous section, the values x and z are interpreted literally, that is, as x and z values. There are two other forms of case statements: casex and casez, that use a different interpretation for x and z values. The syntax is exactly identical to that of a case statement except for the keywords **casex** and **casez**.

In a casez statement, the value z that appears in the case expression and in any case item expression is considered as a don't-care, that is, that bit is ignored (not compared).

In a casex statement, both the values x and z are considered as don't-cares. Here is an example of a casez statement.

```
casez (Mask)
  4'b1??? :  Dbus[4] = 0;
  4'b01?? :  Dbus[3] = 0;
  4'b001? :  Dbus[2] = 0;
  4'b0001 :  Dbus[1] = 0;
endcase
```

The ? character can be used instead of the character z to imply a don't-care. The casez statement example implies that if the first bit of *Mask* is 1 (other bits of *Mask* are ignored), then 0 is assigned to *Dbus*[4], if first bit of *Mask* is 0 and the second bit is 1 (other bits are ignored), then *Dbus*[3] gets assigned the value 0, and so on.

8.7   Loop Statement

There are four kinds of loop statements. These are:

i.   Forever-loop

ii. Repeat-loop

iii. While-loop

iv. For-loop

8.7.1   Forever-loop Statement

The syntax for this form of loop statement is:

```
forever
    procedural_statement
```

This loop statement continuously executes the procedural statement. Thus to get out of such a loop, a disable statement may be used with the procedural statement. Also, some form of timing controls must be used in the procedural statement, otherwise the forever-loop will loop forever in zero delay.

Here is an example of this form of loop statement.

```
initial
  begin
    Clock = 0;
    #5 forever
      # 10 Clock = ~ Clock;
  end
```

This example generates a clock waveform; *Clock* first gets initialized to 0 and stays at 0 until 5 time units. After that *Clock* toggles every 10 time units.

8.7.2   Repeat-loop Statement

This form of loop statement has the form:

```
repeat ( loop_count )
    procedural_statement
```

It executes the procedural statement the specified number of times. If loop count expression is an x or a z, then the loop count is treated as a 0. Here are some examples.

```
repeat (Count)
  Sum = Sum + 10;

repeat (ShiftBy)
  P_Reg = P_Reg << 1;
```

The repeat-loop statement differs from repeat event control. Consider,

```
repeat (Count)            // Repeat-loop statement.
  @ (posedge Clk) Sum = Sum + 1;
```

which means for *Count* times, wait for positive edge of *Clk* and when this occurs, increment *Sum*. Whereas,

```
Sum = repeat (Count) @ (posedge Clk) Sum + 1;
// Repeat event control
```

means to compute *Sum* + 1 first, then wait for *Count* positive edges on *Clk*, then assign to left-hand side.

What does the following mean?

```
repeat (NUM_OF_TIMES) @(negedge ClockZ);
```

It means to wait for *NUM_OF_TIMES* negative clock edges before executing the statement following the repeat statement.

8.7.3   While-loop Statement

The syntax of this form of loop statement is:

```
while ( condition )
  procedural_statement
```

This loop executes the procedural statement until the specified condition becomes false. If the expression is false to begin with, then the procedural statement is never executed. If the condition is an x or a z, it is treated as a 0 (false). Here are some examples.

```
while (By > 0)
  begin
    Acc = Acc << 1;
    By = By - 1;
  end
```

8.7.4   For-loop Statement

This loop statement is of the form:

```
for ( initial_assignment ; condition ; step_assignment )
    procedural_statement
```

A for-loop statement repeats the execution of the procedural statement a certain number of times. The *initial_assignment* specifies the initial value of the loop index. The *condition* specifies the condition when loop execution must stop. As long as the condition is true, the statements in the loop are executed. The *step_assignment* specifies the assignment to modify, typically to increment or decrement, the step count.

```
integer K;

for (K = 0; K < MAX_RANGE; K = K + 1)
  begin
    if (Abus[K] == 0)
      Abus[K] = 1;
    else if (Abus[K] == 1)
      Abus[K] = 0;
    else
      $display ("Abus[K] is an x or a z");
  end
```

8.8   Procedural Continuous Assignment

A procedural continuous assignment is a procedural assignment, that is, it can appear within an always statement or an initial statement. This assignment can override all other assignments to a net or a register. It allows the expression in the assignment to be driven continuously into a register or a net. Note, this is not a continuous assignment; a continuous assignment occurs outside of an initial or an always statement.

There are two kinds of procedural continuous assignments.

    i.   assign and deassign procedural statements: these assign to registers.

> ii.   force and release procedural statements: these assign primarily to nets, though they can also be used for registers.

The assign and force statements are "continuous" in the sense that any change of operand in the right-hand side expression causes the assignment to be re-done while the assign or force is in effect.

The target of a procedural continuous assignment cannot be a part-select or a bit-select of a register.

8.8.1   Assign - deassign

An assign procedural statement overrides all procedural assignments to a register. The deassign procedural statement ends the continuous assignment to a register. The value in the register is retained until assigned again.

```
module DFF (D, Clr, Clk, Q);
  input D, Clr, Clk;
  output Q;
  reg Q;

  always
    @(Clr) begin
      if (! Clr)
        assign Q = 0;      // D has no effect on Q.
      else
        deassign Q;
    end

  always
    @(negedge Clk) Q = D;
endmodule
```

If *Clr* is 0, the assign procedural statement causes *Q* to be stuck at 0 irrespective of any clock edges, that is, *Clk* and *D* have no effect on *Q*. If *Clr* becomes 1, the deassign statement is executed; this causes the override to be removed, so that in the future *Clk* can effect *Q*.

If an assign is applied to an already assigned register, it is deassigned first before making the new procedural continuous assignment. Here is another example.

```
reg [3:0] Pest;
. . .
Pest = 0;
. . .
assign Pest = Hty ^ Mtu;
. . .
assign Pest = 2;   // Will deassign Pest and then assign.
. . .
deassign Pest;    // Pest continues to have value 2.
. . .
assign Pest[2] = 1; /* Error: Bit-select of a register
    cannot be a target of a procedural continuous
    assignment */
```

The second assign statement will cause the first assign to be deassigned before making the next assign. After the deassign is executed, *Pest* continues to keep the value 2 until another assignment to the register occurs.

An assign statement is "continuous" in the sense that after the first assign is executed and before the second assign gets executed, any change on *Hty* or *Mtu* will cause the first assign statement to be reevaluated.

8.8.2   Force - release

The force and release procedural statements are very similar to assign and deassign, except that force and release can be applied to nets as well as to registers.

The force statement, when applied to a register, causes the current value of the register to be overridden by the value of the force expression. When a release on the register is executed, the current value is held in the register unless a procedural continuous assignment was already in effect (at the time the force statement was executed) in which case, the continuous assignment establishes the new value of the register.

A force procedural statement on a net overrides all the drivers for the net until a release procedural statement is executed on that net.

```
wire Prt;
. . .
or #1 (Prt, Std, Dzx);
```

```
initial
  begin
    force Prt = Dzx & Std;
    #5;                       // Wait for 5 time units.
    release Prt;
  end
```

The execution of the force statement causes the value of *Prt* to override the value from the or gate primitive until the release statement is executed, upon which the driver of *Prt* from the or gate primitive takes back its effect. While the force assignment is in effect (first 5 time units), any changes on *Dzx* and *Std* cause the assignment to be executed again.

Here is another example.

```
reg [2:0] Colt;
. . .
Colt = 2;
force Colt = 1;
. . .
release Colt;            // Colt retains value 1.
. . .
assign Colt = 5;
. . .
force Colt = 3;
. . .
release Colt;            // Colt gets the value 5.
. . .
force Colt [1:0] = 3; /* Error: target of a procedural
    continuous assignment cannot be a part-select of a
    register */
```

The first release of *Colt* causes the value of *Colt* to be retained (as 1). This is because there was no procedural continuous assignment applied to the register at the time force was applied. In the latter release statement, *Colt* gets back the value 5 because the procedural continuous assignment on *Colt* becomes active again.

8.9   A Handshake Example

Always statements can be used to capture the behavior of interacting processes, for example, that of interacting finite-state machines. These statements within a module communicate with each other using registers that are visible to all the always statements. It is not recommended to use registers declared within an always statement to pass information between always statements (this is possible through the use of hierarchical path names, described in Chapter 10).

Consider the following example of two interacting processes: *RX*, a receiver, and *MP*, a microprocessor. The *RX* process reads the serial input data and sends a signal *Ready* indicating that the data can be read into the *MP* process. The *MP* process, after it assigns the data to the output, sends an acknowledge signal, *Ack*, back to the *RX* process to begin reading new input data. The block diagram for the two processes is shown in Figure 8-8.

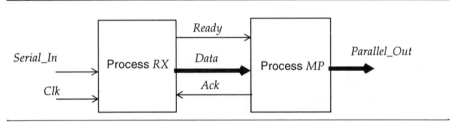

Figure 8-8 Two interacting processes.

The behavior for these two interacting processes is expressed in the following design description.

```
`timescale 1ns / 100ps
module Interacting (Serial_In, Clk, Parallel_Out);
  input Serial_In, Clk;
  output [0:7] Parallel_Out;
  reg [0:7] Parallel_Out;

  reg Ready, Ack;
  wire [0:7] Data;

  `include "Read_Word.v" // Task Read_Word is defined in
                         // this file.
```

```
always
  begin: RX
    Read_Word (Serial_In, Clk, Data);
    // The task Read_Word reads the serial data on every
    // clock cycle and converts to a parallel data in
    // signal Data. It takes 10ns to do this.
    Ready = 1;
    wait (Ack);
    Ready = 0;
    #40;
  end

always
  begin: MP
    #25;
    Parallel_Out = Data;
    Ack = 1;
    #25 Ack = 0;
    wait (Ready);
  end
endmodule
```

The interaction of these two processes via registers *Ready* and *Ack* is shown in the waveforms in Figure 8-9.

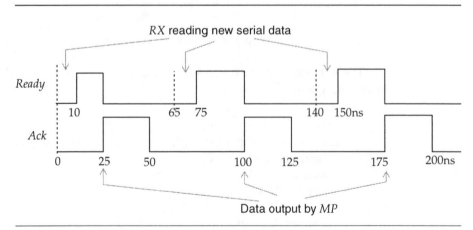

Figure 8-9 Handshaking protocol between the two processes.

8.10   Exercises

1. Which statement executes repeatedly, initial or always statement?

2. What is the difference between a sequential block and a parallel block? Explain using an example. Can a sequential block appear within a parallel block?

3. When is a label required for a block?

4. Is it necessary to specify a delay in an always statement?

5. What is the difference between an intra-statement delay and an inter-statement delay? Explain using an example.

6. How are blocking assignments different from non-blocking assignments?

7. How does the casex statement differ from the case statement?

8. Can a net type (for e.g. a wire) be assigned in an always statement?

9. Generate a clock waveform with an off-period of 5ns and an on-period of 10ns.

10. Express the following always statement using an initial statement and a forever loop statement.

```
always
  @ (Expected or Observed)
    if (Expected !== Observed) begin
      $display ("MISMATCH: Expected = %b, Observed = %b",
              Expected, Observed);
      $stop;
    end
```

11. What are the values of *NextStateA* and *NextStateB* in the following two always statements under the following conditions: *ClockP* has a positive edge at time 5ns; *CurrentState* has a value of 5 prior to the clock edge and changes 3ns after the clock edge to 7?

```
always
  @ (posedge ClockP)
    #7 NextStateA = CurrentState;
```

145

```
always
  @ (posedge ClockP)
    NextStateB = #7 CurrentState;
```

12. Write a model using the behavioral modeling style to describe the following finite state machine.

Inp (Gak)	PresentState	NextState	Output (Zuk)
0	NO_ONE	NO_ONE	0
1	NO_ONE	ONE_ONE	0
0	ONE_ONE	NO_ONE	0
1	ONE_ONE	TWO_ONE	0
0	TWO_ONE	NO_ONE	0
1	TWO_ONE	THREE_ONE	1
0	THREE_ONE	NO_ONE	0
1	THREE_ONE	THREE_ONE	1

13. Describe the behavior of a JK flip-flop using an always statement.

14. Describe the behavior of a circuit that sets the output *Asm* to 1 if a pattern 1011 is found on the input *Usg*. The data on the input is checked on every falling clock edge.

15. Describe the behavior of a majority circuit. The input is a 12-bit vector. If the number of 1's exceeds the number of 0's, the output is set to 1. The input data is checked only when *Data_Ready* is a 1.

❑

Chapter 9

STRUCTURAL MODELING

This chapter describes the structural modeling style of Verilog HDL. Structural modeling is described using:

- Gate instantiation
- UDP instantiation
- Module instantiation

Chapters 5 and 6 have discussed gate-level modeling and UDP modeling. This chapter describes module instantiations.

9.1   Module

A module defines a basic unit in Verilog HDL. It is of the form:

```
module module_name ( port_list );
   Declarations_and_Statements
endmodule
```

The port list gives the list of ports through which the module communicates with the external modules.

9.2   Ports

A port can be declared as input, output or inout. A port by default is a net. However, it can be explicitly declared as a net. An output or an inout port can optionally be redeclared as a reg register. In either the net declaration or the register declaration, the net or register must have the same size as the one specified in the port declaration. Here are some examples of port declarations.

```
module Micro (PC, Instr, NextAddr);
  // Port declarations:
  input [3:1] PC;
  output [1:8] Instr;
  inout [16:1] NextAddr;

  // Redeclarations:
  wire [16:1] NextAddr; // Optional; but if specified must
                        // have same range as in its port declaration.

  reg [1:8] Instr;
  /* Instr has been redeclared as a reg so that it can be
  assigned a value within an always statement or an initial
  statement. */
    . . .
endmodule
```

9.3   Module Instantiation

A module can be instantiated in another module, thus creating hierarchy. A module instantiation statement is of the form:

```
module_name instance_name ( port_associations );
```

Port associations can be by position or by name; however, associations cannot be mixed. A port association is of the form:

```
port_expr               // By position.
.PortName ( port_expr )   // By name.
```

where *port_expr* can be any of the following:

   i.   an identifier (a register or a net)

   ii. a bit-select

   iii. a part-select

   iv. a concatenation of the above

   v. an expression (only for input ports)

In positional association, the port expressions connect to the ports of the module in the specified order. In association by name, the connection between the module port and the port expression is explicitly specified and thus the order of port associations is not important. Here is an example of a full-adder built using two half-adder modules; the logic diagram is shown in Figure 9-1.

```
module HA (A, B, S, C);
  input A, B;
  output S, C;
  parameter AND_DELAY = 1, XOR_DELAY = 2;

  assign #XOR_DELAY   S = A ^ B;
  assign #AND_DELAY   C = A & B;
endmodule

module FA (P, Q, Cin, Sum, Cout);
  input P, Q, Cin;
  output Sum, Cout;
  parameter OR_DELAY = 1;
  wire S1, C1, C2;

  // Two module instantiations:
  HA h1 (P, Q, S1, C1);          // Associating by position.
  HA h2 (.A(Cin), .S(Sum), .B(S1), .C(C2)); // Associating
                                            // by name.
```

```
// Gate instantiation:
or #OR_DELAY O1 (Cout, C1, C2);
endmodule
```

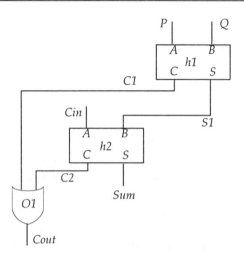

Figure 9-1   A full-adder using half-adder modules.

In the first module instantiation, *HA* is the name of the module, *h1* is the instance name and ports are associated by position, that is, *P* is connected to module (*HA*) port *A*, *Q* is connected to module port *B*, *S1* to *S* and *C1* to module port *C*. In the second instantiation, the port association is by name, that is, the connections between the module (*HA*) ports and the port expressions are specified explicitly.

Here is another example of a module instantiation that uses different forms of port expression.

```
Micro M1   (UdIn[3:0], {WrN, RdN}, Status[0], Status[1],
            & UdOut[0:7], TxData);
```

This instantiation shows that a port expression can be an identifier (*TxData*), a bit-select (*Status*[0]), a part-select (*UdIn*[3:0]), a concatenation ({*WrN*, *RdN*}), or an expression (& *UdOut*[0:7]); an expression can only be connected to an input port.

9.3.1   Unconnected Ports

Unconnected ports in an instantiation can be specified by leaving the port expression blank, such as in the following example.

```
DFF d1 (.Q(QS), .Qbar(), .Data(D),
       .Preset(), .Clock(CK));   // By name.


DFF d2 (QS, , D, , CK);          // By position.
// Output Qbar is not connected.
// Input Preset is open and hence set to value z.
```

In both the instantiations, ports *Qbar* and *Preset* are not connected.

Unconnected module inputs are driven to value **z**. Unconnected module outputs are simply unused.

9.3.2   Different Port Lengths

When a port and the local port expression are of different lengths, port matching is performed by (unsigned) right justification or truncation. Here is an example of port matching.

```
module Child (Pba, Ppy);
  input [5:0] Pba;
  output [2:0] Ppy;
  . . .
endmodule


module Top;
  wire [1:2] Bdl;
  wire [2:6] Mpr;

  Child  C1  (Bdl, Mpr);
endmodule
```

In the module instantiation for *Child*, *Bdl*[2] is connected to *Pba*[0] and *Bdl*[1] is connected to *Pba*[1]. Remaining input ports, *Pba*[5], *Pba*[4], *Pba*[3] are not connected and therefore have the value **z**. Similarly, *Mpr*[6] is connected to *Ppy*[0], *Mpr*[5] is connected to *Ppy*[1] and *Mpr*[4] is connected to *Ppy*[2]. See Figure 9-2.

Figure 9-2   Port matching.

9.3.3   Module Parameter Values

When a module is instantiated in another module, the higher level module can change the value of the parameters in a lower level module. This can be done in two ways.

i.   Defparam statement
ii.   Module instance parameter value assignment

Defparam Statement

A defparam statement is of the form:

```
defparam hier_path_name1 = value1 ,
         hier_path_name2 = value2,. . . ;
```

The hierarchical path names of the parameters in a lower level module can be explicitly set by using such a statement (hierarchical path names are described in the next chapter). Here is an example. Modules *FA* and *HA* have been declared previously in this section.

```
module TOP (NewA, NewB, NewS, NewC);
  input NewA, NewB;
  output NewS, NewC;
  defparam Ha1.XOR_DELAY = 5,
           // Parameter XOR_DELAY in instance Ha1.
           Ha1.AND_DELAY = 2;
           // Parameter AND_DELAY in instance Ha1.

  HA Ha1 (NewA, NewB, NewS, NewC);
endmodule
```

```
module TOP2 (NewP, NewQ, NewCin, NewSum, NewCout);
  input NewP, NewQ, NewCin;
  output NewSum, NewCout;
  defparam Fa1.h1.XOR_DELAY = 2,    // Parameter XOR_DELAY
              // in instance h1 of instance Fa1.
           Fa1.h1.AND_DELAY = 3,    // Parameter AND_DELAY
              // in instance h1 of instance Fa1.
           Fa1.OR_DELAY = 3;        // Parameter OR_DELAY
              // in instance Fa1.

  FA Fa1 (NewP, NewQ, NewCin, NewSum, NewCout);
endmodule
```

Module Instance Parameter Value Assignment

In this method, the new parameter values are specified in the module instantiation itself. Here are the same examples as shown in the previous section, but this time, module instance parameter value assignment is used.

```
module TOP3 (NewA, NewB, NewS, NewC);
  input NewA, NewB;
  output NewS, NewC;

  HA #(5, 2) Ha1 (NewA, NewB, NewS, NewC);
    // First value, 5, is that for parameter AND_DELAY,
    // the first parameter declared in module HA.
    // Second value, 2, is that for parameter XOR_DELAY,
    // the second parameter declared in module HA.
endmodule
```

```
module TOP4 (NewP, NewQ, NewCin, NewSum, NewCout);
  input NewP, NewQ, NewCin;
  output NewSum, NewCout;
  defparam Fa1.h1.XOR_DELAY = 2,    // Parameter XOR_DELAY
              // in instance h1 of instance Fa1.
           Fa1.h1.AND_DELAY = 3;    // Parameter AND_DELAY
              // in instance h1 of instance Fa1.

  FA #(3) Fa1 (NewP, NewQ, NewCin, NewSum, NewCout);
    // Value 3 is the new value for parameter OR_DELAY.
endmodule
```

The order of the parameter values in the instantiation must match the order of parameters declared in the lower-level module. In the module *TOP3*, *AND_DELAY* has been set as 5 and *XOR_DELAY* has been set as 2.

The two modules, *TOP3* and *TOP4*, illustrate the fact that module instance parameter value assignment can be used only to pass parameter values down one level of hierarchy (e.g. *OR_DELAY*), whereas the defparam statement can be used to override parameter values at any level of the hierarchy.

Note that the notation for specifying parameter values appears identical to that of a delay specified in a gate instantiation. This is no case for concern in a module instantiation since delays cannot be specified for a module in the same way as that for a gate instantiation.

Parameter values could also represent sizes. Here is an example that models a generic *M*-by-*N* multiplier.

```
module Multiplier (Opd_1, Opd_2, Result);
  parameter EM = 4, EN = 2; // Default values.
  input [EM:1] Opd_1;
  input [EN:1] Opd_2;
  output [EM+EN : 1] Result;

  assign Result = Opd_1 * Opd_2;
endmodule
```

This parameterized multiplier can now be instantiated in another design. Here is an instantiation of an 8-by-6 multiplier.

```
wire [1:8] Pipe_Reg;
wire [1:6] Dbus;
wire [1:14] Addr_Counter;
 . . .
Multiplier #(8, 6) M1 (Pipe_Reg, Dbus, Addr_Counter);
```

The first value 8 specifies a new value for parameter *EM* and the second value 6 specifies a new value for parameter *EN*.

9.4   External Ports

In the module definition we have seen so far, the port list describes the list of ports visible outside the module. For example,

```
module Scram_A (Arb, Ctrl, Mem_Blk, Byte);
  input [0:3] Arb;
  input Ctrl;
  input [8:0] Mem_Blk;
  output [0:3] Byte;
  . . .
endmodule
```

The module ports are *Arb, Ctrl, Mem_Blk* and *Byte*. These are also the external ports, that is, in an instantiation, the external port names are used to specify the interconnections when associating ports by name. Here is an example of an instantiation of module *Scram_A*.

```
Scram_A SX (.Byte(B1), .Mem_Blk(M1), .Ctrl(C1), .Arb(A1));
```

In module *Scram_A*, the external port names are implicitly specified. Verilog HDL provides an explicit way to specify external port names. This is done by specifying a port of the form:

```
.external_port_name ( internal_port_name )
```

Here is the same example, but this time the external ports are explicitly specified.

```
module Scram_B (.Data(Arb), .Control(Ctrl),
                .Mem_Word(Mem_Blk), .Addr(Byte));
  input [0:3] Arb;
  input Ctrl;
  input [8:0] Mem_Blk;
  output [0:3] Byte;
  . . .
endmodule
```

The module *Scram_B* has external ports specified in this case which are *Data*, *Control*, *Mem_Word* and *Addr*. The port list explicitly shows the connections between the external ports and the internal ports. Note that the external ports need not be declared whereas the internal ports of the module must be declared. The external ports are not visible within the module but are used in a module instantiation whereas internal ports must be declared within the module since they are visible within the module. In a module instantiation, the external ports are used as shown in the following example.

```
Scram_B  S1   (.Addr(A1), .Data(D1), .Control(C1),
                .Mem_Word(M1));
```

The two types of notation cannot be mixed in a port list for a module definition, that is, either all ports in a module definition must have explicit port names specified or none of them must have explicit port names.

External port names are not used in module instantiations if module ports are being connected by position.

An internal port name can not only be an identifier, it can also be one of the following.

- a bit-select
- a part-select
- a concatenation of bit-select, part-select and identifier

Here is an example.

```
module Scram_C (Arb[0:2], Ctrl,
                   {Mem_Blk[0], Mem_Blk[1]}, Byte[3]);
   input [0:3] Arb;
   input Ctrl;
   input [8:0] Mem_Blk;
   output [0:3] Byte;
     . . .
endmodule
```

In the module definition for *Scram_C*, the port list contains a part-select (*Arb*[0:2]), an identifier (*Ctrl*), a concatenation ({*Mem_Blk*[0], *Mem_Blk*[1]}) and a bit-select (*Byte*[3]). In the case where the internal port is a bit-select, part-select or a concatenation, no external port name is implicitly specified. Consequently, in such a module instantiation, module ports must be connected through positional associations. Here is an example of such an instantiation.

```
Scram_C    SYA   (L1[4:6], CL, MMY[1:0], BT);
```

In this instantiation, ports are connected by positional associations; thus, *L1*[4:6] is connected to *Arb*[0:2], *CL* is connected to *Ctrl*, *MMY*[1] is connected to *Mem_Blk*[0], *MMY*[0] to *Mem_Blk*[1], and *BT* is connected to *Byte*[3].

To use association by name in this situation (where an internal port is not an identifier), external port names must be explicitly specified for the ports in the module. This is shown in the following module definition for *Scram_D*.

```
module Scram_D (.Data(Arb[0:2]), .Control(Ctrl),
               .Mem_Word({Mem_Blk[0], Mem_Blk[1]}),
               .Addr(Byte[3]));
   input [0:3] Arb;
   input Ctrl;
   input [8:0] Mem_Blk;
   output [0:3] Byte;
   . . .
endmodule
```

In the instantiation for module *Scram_D*, ports can be connected by position or by name, but not mixed. Here is an example of an instantiation where ports are connected by name.

```
Scram_D    SZ    (.Data(L1[4:6]), .Control(CL),
                 .Mem_Word(MMY[1:0]), .Addr(BT));
```

It is possible for a module to have an external port with no internal port. Here is an example of such a module.

```
module Scram_E (.Data( ), .Control(Ctrl),
               .Mem_Word({Mem_Blk[0], Mem_Blk[1]}),
               .Addr( ));
   input Ctrl;
   input [8:0] Mem_Blk;
   . . .
endmodule
```

Module *Scram_E* has two external ports, *Data* and *Addr*, that are not connected to anything internal to the module.

Can an internal port be connected to more than one external port? Yes, Verilog HDL allows this. Here is an example.

```
module FanOut (.A(CtrlIn), .B(CondOut), .C(CondOut));
  input CtrlIn;
  output CondOut;

  assign CondOut = CtrlIn;
endmodule
```

The internal port *CondOut* is connected to two external ports, *B* and *C*. So the value on *CondOut* appears on both *B* and *C*.

9.5   Examples

Here is an example of a decade counter written in the structural style. The logic diagram is shown in Figure 9-3.

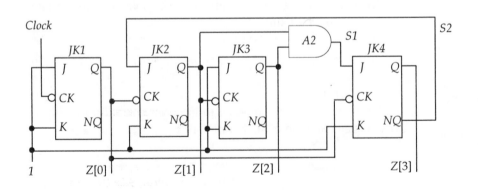

Figure 9-3 A decade counter.

```
module Decade_Ctr (Clock, Z);
  input Clock;
  output [0:3] Z;
  wire S1, S2;

  and A1 (S1, Z[2], Z[1]);// Primitive gate instantiation.

  // Four module instantiations:
  JK_FF JK1 (.J(1'b1), .K(1'b1), .CK(Clock),
             .Q(Z[0]), .NQ()),
        JK2 (.J(S2), .K(1'b1), .CK(Z[0]),
             .Q(Z[1]), .NQ()),
        JK3 (.J(1'b1), .K(1'b1), .CK(Z[1]),
             .Q(Z[2]), .NQ()),
        JK4 (.J(S1), .K(1'b1), .CK(Z[0]),
             .Q(Z[3]), .NQ(S2));
endmodule
```

Notice the usage of constants as values to input ports; also notice the unconnected ports.

Here is another example, this one is that of a three-bit up-down counter shown in Figure 9-4. The structural model follows.

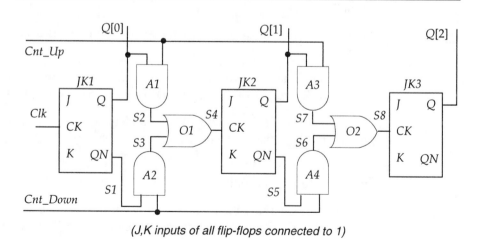

(J,K inputs of all flip-flops connected to 1)

Figure 9-4 A 3-bit up-down counter.

```
module Up_Down (Clk, Cnt_Up, Cnt_Down, Q);
  input Clk, Cnt_Up, Cnt_Down;
  output [0:2] Q;
  wire S1, S2, S3, S4, S5, S6, S7, S8;

  JK_FF  JK1 (1'b1, 1'b1, Clk, Q[0], S1),
         JK2 (1'b1, 1'b1, S4, Q[1], S5),
         JK3 (1'b1, 1'b1, S8, Q[2], );

  and A1 (S2, Cnt_Up, Q[0]),
      A2 (S3, S1, Cnt_Down),
      A3 (S7, Q[1], Cnt_Up),
      A4 (S6, S5, Cnt_Down);

  or  O1 (S4, S2, S3),
      O2 (S8, S7, S6);
endmodule
```

9.6   Exercises

1. What is the difference between a gate instantiation and a module instantiation?

2. What are the values of ports when they are left open, that is, they are not connected?

3. Write a module that instantiates the module *FA* described in Section 9.3 with an *OR_DELAY* of 4, an *XOR_DELAY* of 7 and an *AND_DELAY* of 5.

4. Using the module *FA* described in this chapter, write a structural model for a 4-bit ALU that performs addition and subtraction.

5. Using the module *MUX4x1* described in Section 5.11, write a structural model for a 16-to-1 multiplexer.

6. Describe a generic *N*-bit counter with asynchronous negative level reset. Instantiate this generic counter as a 5-bit counter. Verify this 5-bit counter using a test bench.

❑

Chapter 10

OTHER TOPICS

This chapter describes miscellaneous topics such as functions, tasks, hierarchy, value change dump file and compiler directives.

10.1   Tasks

A task is like a procedure, it provides the ability to execute common pieces of code from several different places in a description. This common piece of code is written as a task (using a task definition) so that it can be called (by a task call) from different places in a design description. A task can contain timing controls, that is, delays, and it can call other tasks and functions as well.

10.1.1   Task Definition

A task is defined using a task definition. It is of the form:

```
task task_id;
  [ declarations ]
  procedural_statement
endtask
```

A task can have zero, one, or more arguments. Values are passed to and from a task through arguments. In addition to input arguments (receive values for a task), a task can have output arguments (return values from a task) and inout arguments as well. A task definition is written within a module declaration. Here is an example of a task definition.

```
module Has_Task;
  parameter MAXBITS = 8;

  task Reverse_Bits;
    input [MAXBITS −1 : 0] Din;
    output [MAXBITS −1 : 0] Dout;
    integer K;

    begin
      for (K = 0; K < MAXBITS; K = K + 1)
        Dout [MAXBITS −K] = Din [K];
    end
  endtask
  . . .
endmodule
```

The inputs and outputs of a task are declared at the beginning of the task. The order of these inputs and outputs specify the order to be used in a task call. Here is another example of a task.

```
task Rotate_Left;
  inout [1:16] In_Arr;
  input [0:3] Start_Bit, Stop_Bit, Rotate_By;
  reg Fill_Value;
  integer Mac1, Mac3;

  begin
    for (Mac3 = 1; Mac3 <= Rotate_By; Mac3 = Mac3 + 1)
    begin
      Fill_Value = In_Arr [Stop_Bit];
```

```
for (Mac1 = Stop_Bit; Mac1 >= Start_Bit + 1;
     Mac1 = Mac1 - 1)
  In_Arr [Mac1] = In_Arr [Mac1 - 1];

  In_Arr [Start_Bit] = Fill_Value;
      end
    end
  endtask
```

Fill_Value is a local register that is directly visible only within the task. The first argument in this task is the inout array, *In_Arr*, followed by the three inputs, *Start_Bit*, *Stop_Bit* and *Rotate_By*.

In addition to the task arguments, a task can reference any variable defined in the module in which the task is declared. An example is shown in the next section.

10.1.2 Task Calling

A task is called (or enabled, as it is said in Verilog HDL) by a task enable statement that specifies the argument values passed to the task and the variables that receive the results. A task enable statement is a procedural statement and can thus appear within an always or an initial statement. It is of the form:

```
task_id [ ( expr1 , expr2 , . . . , exprN ) ] ;
```

The list of arguments must match the order of input, output and inout declarations in the task definition. In addition, arguments are passed by value, not by reference. An important distinction between a task and a procedure in other high-level programming languages such as Pascal is that a task can be called more than once concurrently with each call having its own control. The biggest point to be careful is that a variable declared within a task is static, that is, it never disappears or gets re-initialized. Thus one task call might modify a local variable whose value may be read by another task call.

Here is an example of a task call for the task *Reverse_Bits* whose definition was given in the previous section.

```
// Register declaration:
reg [MAXBITS - 1 : 0] Reg_X, New_Reg;


Reverse_Bits (Reg_X, New_Reg);            // Calling task.
```

The value of *Reg_X* is passed as the input value, that is, to *Din*. The output of the task *Dout* is returned back to *New_Reg*. Note that because a task can contain timing controls, a task may return a value later in time than when it was called.

The output and inout arguments in a task call must be registers because a task enable statement is a procedural statement. In the above example, *New_Reg* must be declared as a register.

Here is an example of a task that references a variable that is not passed in through its argument list. Even though referencing global variables is considered bad programming style, it is sometimes useful as shown in the following example.

```
module Global_Var;
  reg [0:7] RamQ [0:63];
  integer Index;
  reg CheckBit;

  task GetParity;
    input Address;
    output ParityBit;

    ParityBit = ^ RamQ [Address];
  endtask

  initial
    for (Index = 0; Index <= 63; Index = Index + 1) begin
      GetParity (Index, CheckBit);
      $display ("Parity bit of memory word %d is %b.",
                Index, CheckBit);
    end
endmodule
```

The address of the memory *RamQ* is passed as an argument and the memory is referenced directly within the task.

A task can have delays and or it can wait for certain events to occur. However, an assignment to an output argument is not passed to the calling argument until the task exits.

```
module TaskWait;
  reg NoClock;

  task GenerateWaveform;
    output ClockQ;
    begin
      ClockQ = 1;
      #2 ClockQ = 0;
      #2 ClockQ = 1;
      #2 ClockQ = 0;
    end
  endtask

  initial
    GenerateWaveform (NoClock);
endmodule
```

The assignments to *ClockQ* do not appear on *NoClock*, that is, no waveform appears on *NoClock*; only the final assignment to *ClockQ*, which is 0, appears on *NoClock* after the task returns. One way to avoid this problem is to make *ClockQ* as a global register, that is, declare it outside the task.

10.2   Functions

Functions, similar to tasks, also provide the capability to execute common code from different places in a module. The difference from a task is that a function can return only one value, it cannot contain any delays (must execute in zero time) and it cannot call any other task. In addition, a function must have at least one input. No output or inout declarations are allowed in a function. A function may call other functions.

10.2.1   Function Definition

A function definition can appear anywhere in a module declaration. It is of the form:

```
function [ range ] function_id ;
  input_declaration
  other_declarations
  procedural_statement
endfunction
```

An input to the function is declared using the input declaration. If no range is specified with the function definition, then a 1-bit return value is assumed. Here is an example of a function.

```
module Function_Example;
  parameter MAXBITS = 8;

  function [MAXBITS −1 : 0] Reverse_Bits;
    input [MAXBITS −1 : 0] Din;
    integer K;
    begin
      for (K = 0; K < MAXBITS; K = K + 1)
        Reverse_Bits [MAXBITS −K −1] = Din [K];
    end
  endfunction
  . . .
endmodule
```

The name of the function is *Reverse_Bits*. The function returns a vector of size *MAXBITS*. The function has one input, *Din*. K is a local integer.

The function definition implicitly declares a register internal to the function, with the same name and range as the function. A function returns a value by assigning a value to this register explicitly in the function definition. An assignment to this register must therefore be present within a function definition. Here is another example of a function.

```
function Parity;
  input [0:31] Set;
  reg [0:3] Ret;
  integer J;
  begin
    Ret = 0;

    for (J = 0; J <= 31; J = J + 1)
      if (Set[J] == 1)
        Ret = Ret + 1;

    Parity = Ret % 2;
  end
endfunction
```

In this function, *Parity* is the name of the function. Since no size has been specified, the function returns a 1-bit value. *Ret* and *J* are local registers. Note that the last procedural assignment assigns a value to the register which returns the value from the function (a register with the same name as function is implicitly declared within the function).

10.2.2   Function Call

A function call is part of an expression. It is of the form:

```
func_id ( expr1 , expr2 , . . . , exprN )
```

Here is an example of a function call.

```
reg [MAXBITS − 1 : 0] New_Reg, Reg_X;      // Reg declaration.

New_Reg = Reverse_Bits(Reg_X);
  // Function call in right-hand side expression.
```

Similar to a task, all local registers declared within a function definition are static, that is, local registers within a function retain their values between multiple invocations of the function.

10.3   System Tasks and Functions

Verilog HDL provides built-in system tasks and system functions, that is, tasks and functions that are predefined in the language. These are grouped as follows:

   i.   Display tasks

   ii.   File I/O tasks

   iii.   Timescale tasks

   iv.   Simulation control tasks

   v.   Timing check tasks

   vi.   PLA modeling tasks

   vii.   Stochastic modeling tasks

   viii. Conversion functions for reals

   ix.   Probabilistic distribution functions

PLA modeling tasks and stochastic modeling tasks are outside the scope of this book.

10.3.1   Display Tasks

The display system tasks are used for displaying and printing information. These system tasks are further characterized into:

* Display and write tasks.
* Strobed monitoring.
* Continuous monitoring.

Display and Write Tasks

The syntax is of the form:

```
task_name ( format_specification1 , argument_list1 ,
            format_specification2 , argument_list2 ,
            . . . ,
            format_specificationN , argument_listN );
```

where a *task_name* is one of:

$display $displayb $displayh $displayo
$write $writeb $writeh $writeo

The display task prints the specified information to standard output with a end-of-line character, while the write task prints the specified information without an end-of-line character. The following escape sequences can be used for format specification.

```
%h or %H    : hexadecimal
%d or %D    : decimal
%o or %O    : octal
%b or %B    : binary
%c or %C    : ASCII character
%v or %V    : net signal strength
%m or %M    : hierarchical name
%s or %S    : string
%t or %T    : current time format
```

If no format specification exists for an argument, then the default is:

```
decimal     : for $display and $write
binary      : for $displayb and $writeb
octal       : for $displayo and $writeo
hexadecimal : for $displayh and $writeh
```

Special characters can be printed using the following escape sequences.

```
\n          newline
\t          tab
\\          the \ character
\"          the " character
\000        the character with octal value 000
%%          the % character
```

Here are some examples.

```
$display ("Simulation time is %t", $time);
```

```
$display ($time, " : R=%b, S=%b, Q=%b, QB=%b",
     R, S, Q, QB); // Time is displayed in decimal since no
                   // format specification has been specified.

$write ("Simulation time is");
$write (" %t\n", $time);
```

The following is what is displayed when above statements are executed for some values of $time, R, S, Q and QB.

Simulation time is   10

10 : R=1, S=0, Q=0, QB=1

Simulation time is   10

Strobe Tasks

The strobe tasks are:

$strobe   **$strobeb**   **$strobeh** **$strobeo**

These system tasks display the simulation data at the specified time but at the end of the time step. "End of time step" implies that all events have been processed for the specified time step.

```
always
  @ (posedge Rst)
    $strobe ("The flip-flop value is %b at time %t",
              Q, $time);
```

When *Rst* has a positive edge, the $**strobe** task prints the values of *Q* and the current simulation time. Here is the output generated for some values of *Q* and $**time**. Values are printed every time *Rst* has a positive edge.

The flip-flop value is 1 at time   17
The flip-flop value is 0 at time   24
The flip-flop value is 1 at time   26

Format specifications are same as that for display and write tasks.

The strobe task differs from the display task in that the display task is executed at the time the statement is encountered, while the execution of the strobe task is postponed to the end of the time step. The following example helps clarify this further.

```
integer Cool;

initial
  begin
    Cool = 1;
    $display ("After first assignment, Cool has value %d",
             Cool);
    $strobe ("When strobe is executed, Cool has value %d",
             Cool);
    Cool = 2;
    $display ("After second assignment, Cool has value %d",
             Cool);
  end
```

The output produced is:

```
After first assignment, Cool has value       1
After second assignment, Cool has value      2
When strobe is executed, Cool has value      2
```

The first $display task prints the value of *Cool* as 1 (from the first assignment to *Cool*). The second $display task prints the value of *Cool* as 2 (from the second assignment to *Cool*). The $strobe task prints the value of *Cool* as 2, the value it holds at the end of the time step.

Monitor Tasks

The monitor tasks are:

```
$monitor   $monitorb   $monitorh        $monitoro
```

These tasks monitor the specified arguments continuously. Whenever there is a change of value in an argument in the argument list, the entire argument list is displayed at the end of the time step. Here is an example.

```
initial
  $monitor ("At %t, D = %d, Clk = %d ",
    $time, D, Clk, "and Q is %b", Q);
```

When the monitor task is executed, a continuous monitor is set on *D*, *Clk* and *Q*. If any of these change values, the entire argument list is displayed. Here is a sample output for some changes on *D*, *Clk* and *Q*.

```
At        24, D = x, Clk = x and Q is 0
At        25, D = x, Clk = x and Q is 1
At        30, D = 0, Clk = x and Q is 1
At        35, D = 0, Clk = 1 and Q is 1
At        37, D = 0, Clk = 0 and Q is 1
At        43, D = 1, Clk = 0 and Q is 1
```

The format specification is the same as that for a display task. Only one monitor can be active at any time for a particular variable.

Monitoring can be turned on and off by using the following two system tasks.

```
$monitoroff;  // Disables all monitors.
```

```
$monitoron;   // Enables all monitors.
```

These provide a mechanism to control dumping of value changes. The $**monitoroff** task turns off all monitoring so that no more messages are displayed. The $**monitoron** task is used to enable all monitoring.

10.3.2   File I/O Tasks

Opening and Closing Files

A system function $**fopen** is available for opening a file.

```
integer file_pointer = $fopen ( file_name ) ;
  // The $fopen system function returns an integer value
  // (a pointer) to the file.
```

while the following system task can be used to close a file.

```
$fclose (file_pointer);
```

Here is an example of its usage.

```
integer Tq_File;

initial
  begin
    Tq_File = $fopen ("~/jb/div.tq");
    . . .
    $fclose (Tq_File);
  end
```

Writing out to a File

The display, write, strobe and monitor system tasks have a corresponding counterpart that can be used to write information to a file. These are:

```
$fdisplay  $fdisplayb  $fdisplayh  $fdisplayo
$fwrite    $fwriteb    $fwriteh    $fwriteo
$fstrobe   $fstrobeb   $fstrobeh   $fstrobeo
$fmonitor  $fmonitorb  $fmonitorh  $fmonitoro
```

The first argument for all these tasks is a file pointer. Remaining arguments for the task is a list of pairs of format specification followed by an argument list. Here is an example that illustrates this.

```
integer Vec_File;

initial
  begin
    Vec_File = $fopen ("div.vec");
    . . .
    $fdisplay (Vec_File, "The simulation time is %t",
              $time);
      // The first argument Vec_File is the file pointer.
    $fclose (Vec_File);
  end
```

Upon execution of the **$fdisplay** task, the following statement appears in the file "div.vec".

The simulation time is   0

Reading from a File

There are two system tasks available for reading data from a file. These tasks read data from a text file and load the data into memory. These system tasks are:

$readmemb $readmemh

The text file can contain white spaces, comments and binary (for **$readmemb**) or hexadecimal (for **$readmemh**) numbers. Each number is separated by white space. When the system task is executed, each number read is assigned to an address in memory. The beginning address corresponds to the leftmost index of the memory.

```
reg [0:3] Mem_A [0:63];


initial
  $readmemb ("ones_and_zeros.vec", Mem_A);
    // Each number read in is assigned to memory locations
    // starting from 0 to 63.
```

Optionally an explicit address can also be specified in the system task call, such as:

```
$readmemb ("rx.vec", Mem_A, 15, 30);
    // The first number read from the file "rx.vec" is stored
    // in address 15, next one at 16, and so on until
    // address 30.
```

An address may explicitly be given in the text file as well. The address is of the form:

```
@address_in_hexadecimal
```

In such a case, the system task reads the data into the specified address. Subsequent numbers are loaded from that address onwards.

10.3.3   Timescale Tasks

The system task:

$printtimescale

displays the time unit and time precision for the specified module. The **$printtimescale** task with no arguments specified prints the time unit and time precision for the module that contains this task call. If a hierarchical path name to a module is specified as its argument, this system task prints the time unit and precision for the specified module.

$printtimescale;

$printtimescale (*hier_path_to_module*);

Here is a sample output of what appears when these tasks are called.

```
Time scale of (C10) is  100ps /  100ps
Time scale of (C10.INST) is  1us /  100ps
```

The system task:

$timeformat

specifies how the %t format specification must report time information. The task is of the form:

$timeformat (*units_number* , *precision* ,
            suffix , *numeric_field_width*);

where a *units_number* is:

```
0   for 1 s
-1  for 100 ms
```

```
-2  for 10 ms
-3  for 1 ms
-4  for 100 us
-5  for 10us
-6  for 1 us
-7  for 100 us
-8  for 10 ns
-9  for 1 ns
-10 for 100 ps
-11 for 10 ps
-12 for 1 ps
-13 for 100 fs
-14 for 10 fs
-15 for 1 fs
```

The system task call:

```
$timeformat (-4, 3, " ps", 5);
$display ("Current simulation time is %t", $time);
```

will display the %t specifier value in the $display task as:

Current simulation time is 0.051 ps

If no **$timeformat** is specified, %t prints in the smallest precision of all timescales in source.

10.3.4   Simulation Control Tasks

The system task:

```
$finish;
```

makes the simulator exit and return control back to the operating system.

The system task:

```
$stop;
```

causes the simulation to suspend. At this stage, interactive commands may be issued to the simulator. Here is an example of its use.

```
initial #500 $stop;
```

After 500 time units, the simulation stops.

10.3.5   Timing Check Tasks

The system task:

```
$setup ( data_event , reference_event , limit );
```

reports a timing violation if:

```
( time_of_reference_event − time_of_data_event ) < limit
```

An example of this task call is:

```
$setup (D, posedge Ck, 1.0);
```

The system task:

```
$hold ( reference_event , data_event , limit );
```

reports a violation if:

```
(time_of_data_event − time_of_reference_event) < limit
```

Here is an example.

```
$hold (posedge Ck, D, 0.1);
```

The following system task is a combination of the $setup and $hold tasks.

```
$setuphold ( reference_event , data_event , setup_limit ,
             hold_limit );
```

The system task:

```
$width ( reference_event , limit , threshold );
```

reports a violation if:

$$threshold < (\ time\_of\_data\_event -$$
$$time\_of\_reference\_event\ )\ <\ limit$$

The data event is derived from the reference event: it is the reference event with the opposite edge. Here is an example.

$width (negedge Ck, 0.0, 0);

The system task:

$period (reference_event , limit);

reports a violation if:

$$(\ time\_of\_data\_event - time\_of\_reference\_event\ )\ <\ limit$$

The reference event must be an edge-triggered event. The data event is derived from the reference event: it is the reference event with the same edge.

The system task:

$skew (reference_event , data_event , limit);

reports a violation if:

$$time\_of\_data\_event - time\_of\_reference\_event > limit$$

If time of *data_event* is equal to the time of *reference_event*, no violation is reported.

The system task:

$recovery (reference_event , data_event , limit);

reports a timing violation if:

$$(\ time\_of\_data\_event - time\_of\_reference\_event\ )\ <\ limit$$

The reference event must be an edge-triggered event. This system task records the new reference event time before performing the timing check; therefore if the data event and the reference event both occur at the same simulation time, a violation is reported.

The system task:

```
$nochange ( reference_event , data_event , start_edge_offset ,
            end_edge_offset );
```

reports a timing violation if the data event occurs during the specified width of the reference event. The reference event must be an edge-triggered event. The start and stop offsets are relative to the reference event edge. For example,

```
$nochange (negedge Clear, Preset, 0, 0);
```

will report a violation if *Preset* changes while *Clear* is low.

Each of the above system tasks may optionally have a last argument which is a *notifier*. A system task updates a notifier, when there is a timing violation, by changing its value according to the following case statement.

```
case ( notifier )
  'bx : notifier = 'b0;
  'b0 : notifier = 'b1;
  'b1 : notifier = 'b0;
  'bz : notifier = 'bz;
end
```

A notifier can be used to provide information about the violation or propagate an x to the output that reported the violation. Here is an example of a notifier.

```
reg NotifyDin;
. . .
$setuphold (negedge Clock, Din, tSETUP, tHOLD, NotifyDin);
```

In this example, *NotifyDin* is the notifier. If a timing violation occurs, the register *NotifyDin* changes value according to the case statement described earlier for a notifier.

10.3.6 Simulation Time Functions

The following system functions return the simulation time.

- **$time** : Returns the time as an integer in 64 bits scaled to the time unit of the module that invoked it.
- **$stime** : Returns time in 32 bits.
- **$realtime** : Returns time as a real number scaled to the time unit of the module that invokes it.

Here is an example.

```
`timescale 10ns / 1ns
module TB;
  . . .
  initial
    $monitor ("Put_A=%d Put_B=%d", Put_A, Put_B,
              " Get_O=%d", Get_O, "at time %t", $time);
endmodule
```

Here is the output it produces.

```
Put_A=0 Put_B=0 Get_O=0 at time 0
Put_A=0 Put_B=1 Get_O=0 at time 5
Put_A=0 Put_B=0 Get_O=0 at time 16
```

The value returned by **$time** is scaled to the time unit of the module *TB* and then rounded. Note that **$timeformat** decides how the time value is to be printed. Here is another example with its output.

```
initial
  $monitor ("Put_A=%d Put_B=%d", Put_A, Put_B,
            " Get_O=%d", Get_O, "at time %t", $realtime);
```

```
Put_A=0 Put_B=1 Get_O=0 at time 5.2
Put_A=0 Put_B=0 Get_O=0 at time 15.6
```

10.3.7   Conversion Functions

The following system functions are utility functions that convert between number types.

- **$rtoi** (*real_value*) : Converts a real number to an integer by truncating the decimal value.

- **$itor** (*integer_value*) : Converts integer to real.

- **$realtobits** (*real_value*) : Converts a real into 64-bit vector representation of the real number (IEEE 754 representation of the real number).

- **$bitstoreal** (*bit_value*) : Converts a bit pattern into a real number (opposite of **$realtobits**).

10.3.8   Probabilistic Distribution Functions

The function:

```
$random [ ( seed ) ]
```

returns a random number as a 32-bit signed integer based on the value of the seed. The seed (must be a reg, integer or a time register) controls the number that the function returns, that is, a different seed will generate a different random number. If no seed is specified, a random number is generated every time **$random** function is called based on a default seed.

Here is an example.

```
integer Seed, Rnum;
wire Clk;

initial Seed = 12;

always
  @ (Clk) Rnum = $random (Seed);
```

On every edge of *Clk*, **$random** is called which returns a 32-bit signed integer random number.

If a number within a range, say −10 to +10 is desired, the modulus operator can be used to generate such a number as shown in the following example.

```
Rnum = $random (Seed) % 11;
```

Here is an example where the seed is not explicitly specified.

```
Rnum = $random / 2;        // Seed is optional.
```

Note that the sequence of numbers generated is a pseudo-random sequence, that is, the same sequence of numbers is generated for a starting seed value.

The following expression:

```
{$random} % 11
```

returns a random number in the range 0 to 10. The concatenation ({ }) operator interprets the signed integer returned by the $random function as an unsigned number.

The following functions generate pseudo-random numbers according to the probabilistic function specified in the function name.

```
$dist_uniform ( seed , start , end )

$dist_normal ( seed , mean , standard_deviation , upper )

$dist_exponential ( seed , mean )

$dist_poisson ( seed , mean )

$dist_chi_square ( seed , degree_of_freedom )

$dist_t ( seed , degree_of_freedom )

$dist_erlang ( seed , k_stage , mean )
```

All parameters to these functions must be integer values.

10.4   Disable Statement

A disable statement is a procedural statement (hence it can only appear within an always or an initial statement). A disable statement can be used to terminate a task or a block (sequential or parallel) before it completes executing all its statements. It can be used to model hardware interrupts and global resets. It is of the form:

```
disable task_id;
```

```
disable block_id;
```

After a disable statement is executed, execution continues with the next statement following the task call or the block being disabled.

```
begin: BLK_A
  // Stmt1.
  // Stmt2.
  disable BLK_A;
  // Stmt3.
  // Stmt4.
end
// Stmt5.
```

Statements 3 and 4 are never executed. After the disable statement is executed, statement 5 is executed. Here is another example.

```
task Bit_Task;
  begin
    // Stmt 6.
    disable Bit_Task;
    // Stmt 7.
  end
endtask

// Stmt 8.
Bit_Task;        // Task call.
// Stmt 9.
```

When the disable statement is executed, the task is aborted, that is, statement 7 is never executed. Execution continues with the next statement following the task call which in this example is statement 9.

Disabling a task is not recommended, especially if the task returns output values. This is because the language specifies that the values of the output and inout arguments are indeterminate when a task is disabled. A better approach is to disable the sequential block, if any, within the task. For example,

```
task Example;
  output [0:3] Count;
  begin: LOCAL_BLK
    // Stmt 10.
    Count = 10;
    disable LOCAL_BLK;
    // Stmt 11.
  end
endtask
```

When the disable statement gets executed, it causes the sequential block *LOCAL_BLK* to exit. Since this is the only statement in the task, the task exits gracefully and *Count* has its assigned value of 10. If the disable statement were replaced with:

```
disable Example;
```

then after the disable statement gets executed, the value of *Count* is indeterminate.

10.5   Named Events

Consider the following two always statements.

```
reg Ready, Done;

// Get the always statements interacting:
initial
  begin
```

```
      Done = 0;
      #0 Done = 1;
   end

always
   @ (Done) begin
      . . .
      // Finished processing this always statement.
      // Trigger the next always statement.
      // Create an event on Ready:
      Ready = 0;
      #0 Ready = 1;
   end

always
   @ (Ready) begin
      . . .
      // Finished processing this always statement.
      // Create event to trigger previous always statement:
      Done = 0;
      #0 Done = 1;
   end
```

The two assignments in each always statement are needed to ensure that an event is created on *Ready* and *Done*. It appears that the purpose of *Ready* and *Done* are to act only as handshake signals between the two always statements.

Verilog HDL provides an alternate mechanism to achieve this - using *named events*. A named event is yet another data type (the two other data types in the language are the register and the net data types). A named event must be declared before it is used. An example of its declaration is:

```
event Ready, Done;
```

The event declaration declares two named events, *Ready* and *Done*. Having declared a named event, an event can be created using the event trigger statement. Examples of such statements are:

```
-> Ready;
-> Done;
```

Events on named events can be monitored just like events on variables, that is, using the @ mechanism, such as:

```
@ (Done) <do_something>
```

So whenever the event trigger statement for *Done* is executed, an event is said to occur on *Done*, which causes *<do_something>* to execute.

Our simple example of the two always statements can be rewritten using named events as follows.

```
event Ready, Done;

initial
  -> Done;

always
  @ (Done) begin

    . . .
    // Trigger the next always statement.
    // Create an event on Ready:
    -> Ready;
  end

always
  @ (Ready) begin

    . . .
    // Create event to trigger previous always statement:
    -> Done;
  end
```

A state machine can also be described using events. Here is an example of an asynchronous state machine.

```
event State1, State2, State3;

// Reset state:
initial
  begin
    // Reset state logic here.
    -> State1;
  end
```

```
always
  @ (State1) begin
    // State1 logic here.
    -> State2;          // Create event on State2.
  end

always
  @ (State2) begin
    // State2 logic here.
    -> State3;          // Create event on State3.
  end

always
  @ (State3) begin
    // State3 logic here. It can have statements such as:
    if (InputA)
      -> State2;        // Create event on State2.
    else
      -> State1;        // Create event on State1.
  end
```

The initial statement describes the reset logic. Upon completion, it triggers the second always statement. The execution of the last statement in this always statement causes an event to occur on *State2*; this causes the third always statement to execute and subsequently the fourth always statement executes. In the last always statement, an event is made to occur either on *State2* or on *State1* depending on the value of *InputA*.

10.6   Mixing Structure with Behavior

In previous chapters, we discussed the various forms of modeling. Verilog HDL allows all these modeling styles to be combined in a single module. The syntax of a module is:

```
module module_name ( port_list );
  Declarations:
    Input, output and inout declarations.
    Net declarations.
    Reg declarations.
```

```
    Parameter declarations.

    Initial statement.
    Gate instantiation statement.
    Module instantiation statement.
    UDP instantiation statement.
    Always statement.
    Continuous assignment.
endmodule
```

Here is an example of a mixed style description.

```
module MUX2x1 (Ctrl, A, B, Ena, Z);
  // Input declaration:
  input Ctrl, A, B, Ena;
  // Output declaration:
  output Z;
  // Wire declaration:
  wire Mot, Not_Ctrl;
  // Net declaration assignment:
  wire Z = Ena == 1 ? Mot : 'bz;

  // Gate instantiations:
  not (Not_Ctrl, Ctrl);
  or (Mot, Ta, Tb);

  // Continuous assignments:
  assign Ta = A & Ctrl;
  assign Tb = B & Not_Ctrl;
endmodule
```

The module contains a mix of built-in logic gates (structural components) and continuous assignments (dataflow behavior).

10.7   Hierarchical Path Name

Every identifier in Verilog HDL has a unique hierarchical path name. This hierarchical path name is formed by using names separated by a period (.) character. A new hierarchy is defined by:

i.   Module instantiation.

ii.   Task definition.

iii.   Function definition.

iv.   Named block.

The complete path name of any identifier starts with the top-level module (a module that is not instantiated by anybody else). This path name can be used in any level in a description. Here is an example. Figure 10-1 shows the hierarchy.

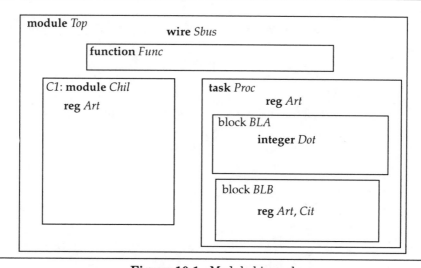

Figure 10-1   Module hierarchy.

```
module Top;
  wire Sbus;

  function Func . . .
      . . .
  endfunction

  task Proc
      . . .
    reg Art;

    begin: BLA
      integer Dot;
```

```
          .  .  .
      end

    begin: BLB
      reg Art, Cit;
        .  .  .
      end
    endtask

    Chil C1 (. . .); // A module instantiation.
  endmodule  // Module Top.

  module Chil;
    reg Art;
      .  .  .
  endmodule
```

The hierarchical names in this example are:

```
Top.C1.Art
Top.Proc.Art
Top.Proc.BLB.Art
Top.Proc.BLA.Dot
Top.Proc.BLB.Cit
Top.Sbus
```

These hierarchical names allow free data access to any item from any level in the hierarchy. The value can not only be read, but can also be updated from any level of the hierarchy.

A lower level module can reference an item in a module above it (called upward referencing) or below it (downward referencing) in its hierarchy by qualifying the variable with the module instance name. This is of the form:

```
module_instance_name . variable_name
```

For downward path referencing, the model instance must be at the same level as the lower-level module. Here is an example.

```
module Top;
  wire Sbus;

  Chil C1 (. . .);      // A module instantiation.

  $display (C1.Art); // Downward referencing.
endmodule

module Chil;
  reg Art;

  . . .
endmodule
```

10.8   Sharing Tasks and Functions

One approach to share tasks and functions among different modules is to write the definitions of the shared tasks and functions in a text file, and then include these in the required module using the `include compiler directive. Assume that we have the following function and task definitions in a file "share.h".

```
function SignedPlus;
  . . .
endfunction

function SignedMinus;
  . . .
endfunction

task PresetClear;
  . . .
endtask
```

Here is how the file can be used in a module.

```
module SignedAlu (A, B, Operation, Z);
  input [0:3] A, B;
  input Operation;
  output [0:3] Z;
  reg [0:3] Z;

  // Include the definitions of the shared functions.
  `include "share.h"

  always
    @ (A or B or Operation)
      if (Operation)
        Z = SignedPlus (A, B);
      else
        Z = SignedMinus (A, B);
endmodule
```

Note that the `include directive must be present within the module declaration since the task and function definitions in the file "share.h" are not bounded by a module declaration.

An alternate way to share functions and tasks is to define the shared tasks and functions within a module. And then refer to the required task or function in a different module using a hierarchical name. Here is the same example as above, but this time the task and function definitions appear within a module declaration.

```
module Share;
  function SignedPlus;

    . . .

  endfunction

  function SignedMinus;

    . . .

  endfunction

  task PresetClear;

    . . .

  endtask
endmodule
```

Here is how the shared functions can be referenced in a different module.

```
module SignedAlu2 (A, B, Operation, Z);
  input [0:3] A, B;
  input Operation;
  output [0:3] Z;
  reg [0:3] Z;

  always
    @ (A or B or Operation)
     if (Operation)
       Z = Share.SignedPlus (A, B);
     else
       Z = Share.SignedMinus (A, B);
endmodule
```

10.9   Value Change Dump (VCD) File

A value change dump (VCD) file contains information about value changes on specified variables in design. Its main purpose is to provide information
for other post-processing tools.

The following system tasks are provided to create and direct information
into a VCD file.

i.   **$dumpfile** : This system task specifies the name of the dump file.
       For example,

```
$dumpfile ("uart.dump");
```

ii. **$dumpvars** : This system task specifies the variables whose val-
       ue changes are to be dumped into the dump file.

```
$dumpvars;
    // With no arguments, it specifies to dump all
    // variables in the design.
```

```
$dumpvars (level, module_name);
    // Dumps variables in specified module and in all
    // modules the specified number of levels below.
```

```
$dumpvars (1, UART);
  // Dumps variables only in UART module.

$dumpvars (2, UART);
  // All variables in UART and in all modules one
  // level below.

$dumpvars (0, UART);
  // Level 0 causes all variables in UART and all
  // variables in all module instances below UART.

$dumpvars (0, P_State, N_State);
  // Dumps info about P_State and N_State variables.
  // The level number is not relevant in this case, but
  // must be given.

$dumpvars (3, Div.Clk, UART);
  // The level number applies only to modules, in this
  // case, only to UART, that is, all variables in UART
  // and two levels below. Also dumps value changes on
  // variable Div.Clk.
```

iii. **$dumpoff** : This system task causes the dumping tasks to be suspended.

```
$dumpoff;
```

iv. **$dumpon** : This system task causes all dumping tasks to resume. The syntax is:

```
$dumpon;
```

v. **$dumpall** : This system tasks dumps the values of all specified variables at that time, that is at the time it is executed. The syntax is:

```
$dumpall;
```

vi. **$dumplimit** : This system task specifies the maximum size (in bytes) for a VCD file. Dumping stops when this limit is reached. For example,

```
$dumplimit (1024);     // VCD file is of maximum
                       // 1024 bytes.
```

vii. **$dumpflush** : This system task flushes data in the operating system VCD file buffer to be stored in the VCD file. After the execution of the system task, dumping resumes as before.

```
$dumpflush;
```

10.9.1   An Example

Here is an example of an up-down counter that counts between 5 and 12.

```
module CountUpDown (Clk, Count, Up_Down);
  input Clk, Up_Down;
  output [0:3] Count;
  reg [0:3] Count;

  initial Count = 'd5;

  always
    @ (posedge Clk) begin
      if (Up_Down)
        begin
          Count = Count + 1;

          if (Count > 12)
            Count = 12;
        end
      else
        begin
          Count = Count - 1;

          if (Count < 5)
            Count = 5;
        end
```

```
          end
    endmodule

    module Test;
      reg Clock, UpDn;
      wire [0:3] Cnt_Out;
      parameter ON_DELAY = 1, OFF_DELAY = 2;

      CountUpDown C1 (Clock, Cnt_Out, UpDn);

      always
        begin
          Clock = 1;
          #ON_DELAY;
          Clock = 0;
          #OFF_DELAY;
        end

      initial
        begin
          UpDn = 0;
          #50 UpDn = 1;
          #100 $dumpflush;
          $stop;          // Stops the simulation.
        end

      initial
        begin
          $dumpfile ("count.dump");
          $dumplimit (4096);
          $dumpvars (0, Test);
          $dumpvars (0, C1.Count, C1.Clk, C1.Up_Down);
        end
    endmodule
```

10.9.2 Format of VCD File

The VCD file is an ASCII file. It has the following information:

- Header information: Gives date, simulator version and timescale unit.

- Node information: Definition of the scope and type of variables being dumped.
- Value changes: Actual value changes with time. Absolute simulation times are recorded.

The VCD file produced is shown in Figure 10-2.

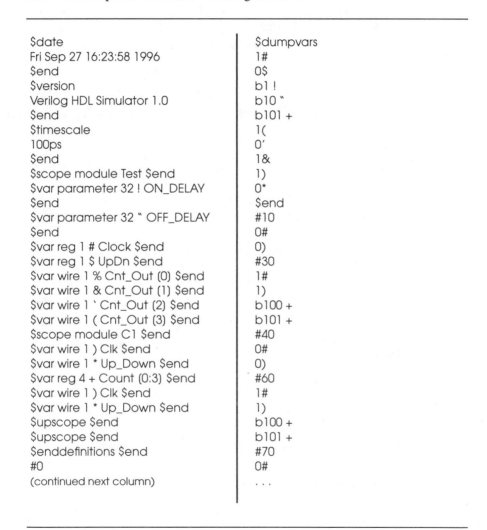

```
$date                               $dumpvars
Fri Sep 27 16:23:58 1996            1#
$end                                0$
$version                            b1 !
Verilog HDL Simulator 1.0           b10 "
$end                                b101 +
$timescale                          1(
100ps                               0'
$end                                1&
$scope module Test $end             1)
$var parameter 32 ! ON_DELAY        0*
$end                                $end
$var parameter 32 " OFF_DELAY       #10
$end                                0#
$var reg 1 # Clock $end             0)
$var reg 1 $ UpDn $end              #30
$var wire 1 % Cnt_Out (0) $end      1#
$var wire 1 & Cnt_Out (1) $end      1)
$var wire 1 ` Cnt_Out (2) $end      b100 +
$var wire 1 ( Cnt_Out (3) $end      b101 +
$scope module C1 $end               #40
$var wire 1 ) Clk $end              0#
$var wire 1 * Up_Down $end          0)
$var reg 4 + Count (0:3) $end       #60
$var wire 1 ) Clk $end              1#
$var wire 1 * Up_Down $end          1)
$upscope $end                       b100 +
$upscope $end                       b101 +
$enddefinitions $end                #70
#0                                  0#
(continued next column)             . . .
```

Figure 10-2 A VCD file.

10.10   Specify Block

The delays that we have discussed so far such as gate delays and net delays are distributed delays. Delays for paths in a module, called module path delays, can be specified using a specify block. In general, a specify block can be used for the following.

    i.   To declare paths between a source and a destination.

    ii. To assign delay to these paths.

    iii. To perform timing checks for the module.

A specify block appears within a module declaration. It is of the form:

```
specify
  spec_param_declarations
  path_declarations
  system_timing_checks
endspecify
```

A specparam (or a specify parameter) declaration declares a parameter for use within the specify block. Here is an example.

```
specparam tSETUP = 20, tHOLD = 25;
```

Three kinds of module paths can be described within a specify block. These are:

- Simple path.
- Edge-sensitive path.
- State-dependent path.

A simple path is declared using one of the following two forms.

```
source *> destination
  // Specifies a full connection: each bit in source
  // connects to all bits in destination.

source => destination
  // Specifies a parallel connection: every bit in source
  // connects to exactly one bit in destination.
```

Here are some examples.

```
input Clock;
input [7:4] D;
output [4:1] Q;


(Clock => Q[1]) = 5;
  // Delay from input Clock to Q[1] is 5.

(D *> Q) = (tRISE, tFALL);
  /* Paths are:
      D[7] to Q[4]
      D[7] to Q[3]
      D[7] to Q[2]
      D[7] to Q[1]
      D[6] to Q[4]
      . . .
      D[4] to Q[1]
  */
```

In an edge-sensitive path, the path is described with respect to an edge on the source. For example,

```
(posedge Clock => (Qb +: Da)) = (2:3:2);
  /* The path delay is from the positive edge of Clock to Qb.
     The data path is from Da to Qb and Da does not get
     inverted as it propagates to Qb. */
```

A state-dependent path specifies a path delay under some condition when it is true. For example,

```
if (Clear)
  (D => Q) = (2.1, 4.2);
    // Only if Clear is true, use the delay for the
    // specified path.
```

Here is a list of timing check system tasks that can be used within a specify block.

```
$setup          $hold
$setuphold      $period
$skew           $recovery
$width          $nochange
```

Here is an example of a specify block.

```
specify
  // Specify parameters:
  specparam tCLK_Q = (5:4:6);
  specparam tSETUP = 2.8, tHOLD = 4.4;

  // Path delays with path specifications:
  (Clock *> Q) = tCLK_Q;
  (Data *> Q) = 12;
  (Clear, Preset *> Q) = (4, 5);

  // Timing check:
  $setuphold (negedge Clock, Data, tSETUP, tHOLD);
endspecify
```

Along a module path, only pulses that are longer than the path delay propagate to the output. However, this can additionally be controlled by using a special specify block parameter called **PATHPULSE**$. In addition to specifying the pulse width range for which a pulse is rejected, it can also be used to specify a pulse width range that will cause an **x** to appear at the end of the path. A simple form of this parameter specification is:

```
PATHPULSE$ = ( reject_limit , [ , error_limit ] );
```

If a pulse width is less than the *reject_limit*, the pulse does not propagate to output. If a pulse width is less than the *error_limit* (same as *reject_limit* if not specified) but greater than the *reject_limit*, an **x** is generated at the target of the path.

A pulse limit can be specified for a specific path as well by using a modified **PATHPULSE**$ parameter of the form:

```
PATHPULSE$ input_terminal$ output_terminal
```

Here is an example of a specify block.

```
specify
  specparam PATHPULSE$ = (1, 2);
    // Reject limit = 1, Error limit = 2.
  specparam PATHPULSE$Data$Q = 6;
    // Reject limit = Error limit = 6, on path from Data to Q.
endspecify
```

10.11 Strengths

In addition to the four basic values in Verilog HDL, 0, 1, x and z, additional attributes to these values such as drive strength and charge strength can be specified.

10.11.1 Drive Strength

A drive strength can be specified for the following:

i.   A net in a net declaration assignment.

ii. Output terminal of a primitive gate instance.

iii. In a continuous assignment.

A drive strength specification has two values, one is the strength value when the net is assigned a value 1, the second is the strength value when the net is assigned a value 0. It is of the form:

(*strength_for_1* , *strength_for_0*)

The order of the values is not important. For an assignment of value 1, only the following strengths are allowed.

- **supply1**
- **strong1**
- **pull1**
- **weak1**
- **highz1** (not allowed for gate primitives)

For an assignment of value 0, the following strengths are allowed.

- **supply0**

- **strong0**
- **pull0**
- **weak0**
- **highz0** (not allowed for gate primitives)

The default strength specification is (**strong0**, **strong1**).

Here are some examples.

```
// Strength for a net:
wire (pull1, weak0) #(2, 4) Lrk = Pol && Ord;
   // Strengths can be specified only for scalar nets of type:
   // wire, wand, wor, tri, triand, trior, trireg,
   // tri0, tri1.

// Strength for an output terminal of a gate primitive:
nand (pull1, strong0) #(3:4:4) A1 (Mout, MinA, MinB, MinC);
   // Drive strengths can only be specified for the following
   // gate primitives: and, or, xor, nand, nor, xnor, buf,
   // bufif0, bufif1, not, notif0, notif1, pulldown, pullup.

// Strength in a continuous assignment:
assign (weak1, pull0) #2.56 Wrt = Ctrl;
```

The strength of a net can be printed using the %v format specification in a display task. For example,

```
$display ("Prq is %v", Prq);
```

produces:

Prq is We1

10.11.2 Charge Strength

A trireg net can optionally have a charge strength specified as well. This charge strength specifies the relative size of the capacitance associated with the net. It is one of:

- **small**
- **medium** (default, if not specified)

- **large**

In addition, a charge decay time can be specified for a trireg net. Here is an example.

```
trireg (small) #(5, 4, 20) Tro;
```

The trireg net *Tro* has a **small** capacitance. The rise delay is 5 time units, the fall delay is 4 time units and the charge decay time (the charge decays when the net is in high-impedance) is 20 time units.

10.12 Race Condition

If a delay is not used in a continuous assignment or in an always statement, a race condition can occur due to zero delay. This is because Verilog HDL does not define how events, which occur at the same time, are ordered for simulation.

Here is a simple example that illustrates this fact about zero delays using non-blocking assignments.

```
begin
  Start <= 0;
  Start <= 1;
end
```

Both values 0 and 1 get scheduled to be assigned to *Start* at the end of the time step. Depending on how the events are ordered (internal to a simulator), the result on *Start* may be a 0 or a 1.

Here is another example that shows a race condition due to event ordering.

```
initial
  begin
    Pal = 0;
    Ctrl = 1;
    #5 Pal = 1;
    Ctrl = 0;
  end
```

```
always
  @ (Cot or Ctrl) begin
    $display ("The value of Cot at time", $time, " is ",
              Cot);
  end

assign Cot = Pal;
```

When *Pal* and *Ctrl* are assigned values in the initial statement at time 0, the continuous assignment and the always statement are both ready for execution. Which one should be executed first? The Verilog language does not define this order. If the continuous assignment executes first, *Cot* will get 0, which in turn will trigger the always statement. But since it is already ready for execution, nothing is done. The always statement gets executed which displays the value of 0 for *Cot*.

If we assume that the always statement executes first, the current value of *Cot* is printed (the continuous assignment has not yet been executed), and then the continuous assignment gets executed which updates the value of *Cot*.

Therefore be careful when dealing with zero delay assignments. Here is another example of a race condition.

```
always @ (posedge GlobalClk)
  RegB = RegA;

always @ (posedge GlobalClk)
  RegC = RegB;
```

The language does not define which always statement is to be executed first when there is a positive edge on *GlobalClk*. If the first always statement is executed, *RegB* will get the value of *RegA* immediately. Subsequently when the second always statement executes, *RegC* will get the latest value of *RegB* (the one assigned in the first always statement).

If the second always statement executes first, *RegC* will get the old value of *RegB* (*RegB* has not yet been assigned), and subsequently *RegB* will be assigned the value of *RegA*. So depending on which always statement executes first, *RegC* will have a different value. The problem occurs because the procedural assignment occurs instantaneously, that is, without any delay. One way to avoid the problem is to insert intra-statement delays. A better approach is to use non-blocking assignment statements. This is shown next.

```
always @(posedge GlobalClk)
  RegB <= RegA;

always @(posedge GlobalClk)
  RegC <= RegB;
```

When communicating information via variables from one always statement to another, use non-blocking assignments when assigning to the variables to avoid race conditions.

10.13 Exercises

1. Can a function call a task?

2. Can a task have delays?

3. Can a function have zero input parameters?

4. What is the difference between $display and $write system tasks?

5. What is the difference between $strobe and $monitor system tasks?

6. Write a function that performs a BCD (binary coded decimal) to 7-segment decoding.

7. Write a function that converts a four-character string that contains only decimal digits to an integer value. For example, if *MyBuffer* contains the string "4298", convert it to an integer *MyInt* that has the value 4298.

8. Does Verilog HDL have a capability to read files other than using the $readmemb and $readmemh system tasks?

9. What is the difference between $stop and $finish system tasks?

10. Write a task that dumps the contents of a memory starting from a specified begin and end locations.

11. What is a notifier? Give an example of its use.

12. How would you load a memory from locations 0 through 15. Hexadecimal values are read from a text file "ram.txt".

13. Write a task that models the behavior of an asynchronous preset clear positive edge triggered counter.

14. What statement can be used to return from a task?

15. What system task impacts how the $time value is to be printed?

16. What mechanism is used to specify a pulse rejection limit?

17. Write a function that performs an arithmetic shift of a 10-bit vector.

18. Show how a disable statement can be used to emulate the behavior of the "continue" and "break" statements of the C programming language.

19. Given an absolute UNIX path name of a file, say of form *ID1/D2/D3/ fileA*, write the following functions:
    - *GetDirectoryName*: returns the directory of file (i.e. */D1/D2/D3*)
    - *GetBaseName*: returns the name of file (i.e. *fileA*)
    Assume that the maximum number of characters in the path name can be at most 512 characters.

□

Chapter 11

VERIFICATION

This chapter describes techniques for writing test benches. A test bench is a program used for exercising and verifying the correctness of a design. Verilog HDL provides powerful constructs that can be used to describe test benches.

11.1   Writing a Test Bench

A test bench has three main purposes.

    i.   To generate stimulus for simulation (waveforms).

    ii.   To apply this stimulus to the module under test and collect output responses.

    iii. To compare output responses with expected values.

Verilog HDL provides a large number of ways to write a test bench. In this chapter, we explore some of these. A typical test bench is of the form:

```
module Test_Bench;
  // A test bench typically has no inputs and outputs.
  Local_reg_and_net_declarations
  Generate_waveforms_using_initial_&_always_statements
  Instantiate_module_under_test
  Monitor_output_and_compare_with_expected_values
endmodule
```

Stimulus is automatically applied to the module under test by instantiating it in the testbench module.

11.2   Waveform Generation

There are two main approaches to generate stimulus values.

i. Create waveforms and apply stimulus at certain discrete time intervals.

ii. Generate stimulus based on the state of the module, that is, based on the output response of the module.

Two types of waveforms are typically needed. One is a repetitive pattern, for example, a clock, and the other is a specified set of values.

11.2.1   A Sequence of Values

The best way to generate a sequence of values is to use an initial statement. Here is an example.

```
initial
  begin
    Reset = 0;
    #100 Reset = 1;
    #80 Reset = 0;
    #30 Reset = 1;
  end
```

The waveform generated is shown in Figure 11-1. The assignment statements in the initial statement use delay controls to generate a waveform. Alternately,

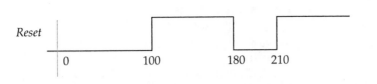

Figure 11-1 Waveform generated using initial statement.

intra-statement delays can also be used to generate a waveform as shown in the following example.

```
initial
  begin
    Reset = 0;
    Reset = #100 1;
    Reset = #80 0;
    Reset = #30 1;
  end
```

Since blocking procedural assignments are used, the delays in the above statements are relative delays. If absolute delays are preferred to be used, non-blocking procedural assignments can be used with intra-statement delays, as shown in the following example.

```
initial
  begin
    Reset <= 0;
    Reset <= #100 1;
    Reset <= #180 0;
    Reset <= #210 1;
  end
```

The waveforms produced for all the three initial statements are identical to the one shown in Figure 11-1.

To repeat a sequence of values, use an always statement instead of an initial statement; this is because an initial statement executes only once while an always statement executes repeatedly. Figure 11-2 shows the waveform created for the following example with an always statement.

```
parameter REPEAT_DELAY = 35;
integer CoinValue;

always
  begin
    CoinValue = 0;
    #7 CoinValue = 25;
    #2 CoinValue = 5;
    #8 CoinValue = 10;
    #6 CoinValue = 5;
    #REPEAT_DELAY;
  end
```

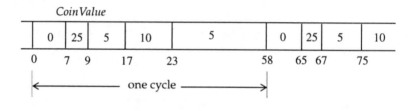

Figure 11-2 A repetitive sequence generated using an always statement.

11.2.2 Repetitive Patterns

It appears that a repetitive pattern can simply be created by having a continuous assignment of the form:

```
assign #(PERIOD/2)   Clock = ~ Clock;
```

But this is not completely correct. The problem is that since *Clock* is a net (only a net can be assigned in a continuous assignment), its initial value is an z and ~z is x and ~x is x. Therefore the *Clock* gets stuck at the value x forever.

What is needed is a way to initialize the *Clock*. This can be done using an initial statement.

```
initial
  Clock = 0;
```

But now *Clock* has to be a register data type (since only register data types can be assigned values in an initial statement), and therefore the continuous assignment needs to be changed to an always statement. Here is a complete clock generator module.

```
module Gen_Clk_A (Clk_A);
  output Clk_A;
  reg Clk_A;
  parameter tPERIOD = 10;

  initial
    Clk_A = 0;

  always
    #(tPERIOD/2)    Clk_A = ~ Clk_A;
endmodule
```

The waveform produced is shown in Figure 11-3.

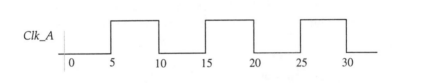

Figure 11-3 Periodic clock.

An alternate way of generating a clock is shown next.

```
module Gen_Clk_B (Clk_B);
  output Clk_B;
  reg Start;

  initial
    begin
      Start = 1;
      #5 Start = 0;
    end

  nor #2 (Clk_B, Start, Clk_B);
```

endmodule
// Generates a clock with on-off width of 2.

The initial statement sets *Start* to 1, which forces the output of the nor gate to be a 0 (gets out of **x** value). After 5 time units, when *Start* goes to 0, the inversion of the nor gate produces the clock with an on-off period of 4 time units. The waveform produced is shown in Figure 11-4.

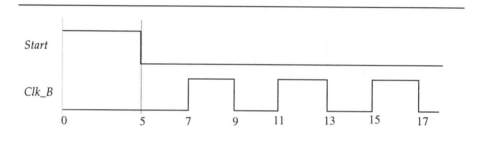

Figure 11-4   A controlled clock.

If a clock with different on-off duration is required, this can be modeled using an always statement as shown in the next model.

```
module Gen_Clk_C (Clk_C);
  parameter tON = 5, tOFF = 10;
  output Clk_C;
  reg Clk_C;

  always
    begin
      #tON   Clk_C = 0;
      #tOFF  Clk_C = 1;
    end
endmodule
```

No initialization is necessary in this case since the values 0 and 1 are being explicitly assigned. Figure 11-5 shows the waveform generated for this module.

To generate a varying on-off period clock after a start-up delay, a forever loop in an initial statement can be used.

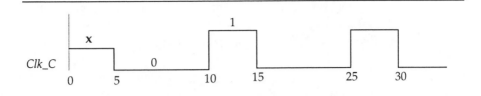

Figure 11-5 Varying on-off period.

```
module Gen_Clk_D (Clk_D);
  output Clk_D;
  reg Clk_D;
  parameter START_DELAY = 5, LOW_TIME = 2, HIGH_TIME = 3;

  initial
    begin
      Clk_D = 0;
      # START_DELAY;

      forever
        begin
          # LOW_TIME;
          Clk_D = 1;
          # HIGH_TIME;
          Clk_D = 0;
        end
    end
endmodule
```

Figure 11-6 shows the waveforms produced.

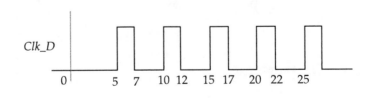

Figure 11-6 Clock with start-up delay.

To generate a fixed number of clock pulses, a repeat loop can be used. Here is a parameterized clock module that generates such a sequence of pulses. Even the on-off delays are parameterized.

```
module Gen_Clk_E (Clk_E);
  output Clk_E;
  reg Clk_E;
  parameter Tburst = 10, Ton = 2, Toff = 5;

  initial
    begin
      Clk_E = 1'b0;

      repeat (Tburst)
        begin
          # Toff Clk_E = 1'b1;
          # Ton  Clk_E = 1'b0;
        end
    end
endmodule
```

Module *Gen_Clk_E* can be instantiated with different parameter values for *Tburst*, *Ton* and *Toff*.

```
module Test;
  wire Clk_Ea, Clk_Eb, Clk_Ec;

  Gen_Clk_E     G1    (Clk_Ea);
    // Burst of 10 pulses, on-time of 2 and off-time of 5.

  Gen_Clk_E     #(5, 1, 3) (Clk_Eb);
    // Burst of 5 pulses, on-time of 1 and off-time of 3.

  Gen_Clk_E     #(25, 8, 10) (Clk_Ec);
    // Burst of 25 pulses, on-time of 8 and off-time of 10.
endmodule
```

The waveforms on *Clk_Eb* is shown in Figure 11-7.

A clock that is phase-delayed from another clock can be generated by using a continuous assignment. Figure 11-8 shows the generated waveforms for

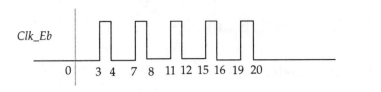

Figure 11-7 Fixed number of clock pulses.

the following module that generates two clocks, one of which is phase-delayed from the other.

```
module Phase (Master_Clk, Slave_Clk);
  output Master_Clk, Slave_Clk;
  reg Master_Clk;
  wire Slave_Clk;
  parameter tON = 2, tOFF = 3, tPHASE_DELAY = 1;

  always
    begin
      #tON   Master_Clk = 0;
      #tOFF  Master_Clk = 1;
    end

  assign #tPHASE_DELAY  Slave_Clk = Master_Clk;
endmodule
```

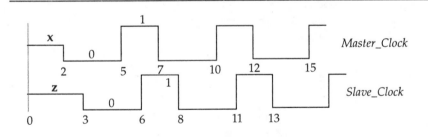

Figure 11-8 Phase-delayed clocks.

215

11.3   Testbench Examples

11.3.1   A Decoder

Here is a description of a 2-to-4 decoder and its test bench. Output is printed any time there is a change of value on either the input or the output.

```
`timescale 1ns / 1ns
module Dec2x4 (A, B, Enable, Z);
  input A, B, Enable;
  output [0:3] Z;
  wire Abar, Bbar;

  not # (1, 2)
    V0 (Abar, A),
    V1 (Bbar, B);

  nand #(4, 3)
    N0 (Z[0], Enable, Abar, Bbar),
    N1 (Z[1], Enable, Abar, B),
    N2 (Z[2], Enable, A, Bbar),
    N3 (Z[3], Enable, A, B);
endmodule

module Dec_Test;
  reg Da, Db, Dena;
  wire [0:3] Dz;

  // Module under test:
  Dec2x4 D1 (Da, Db, Dena, Dz);

  // Generate waveforms:
  initial
    begin
      Dena = 0;
      Da = 0;
      Db = 0;
      #10 Dena = 1;
      #10 Da = 1;
      #10 Db = 1;
```

```
        #10 Da = 0;
        #10 Db = 0;
        #10 $stop;
      end

  // Print results:
  always
    @ (Dena or Da or Db or Dz)
      $display ("At time %t, input is %b%b%b, output is %b",
            $time, Da, Db, Dena, Dz);
endmodule
```

Here is the output produced when this test bench is executed.

At time	4, input is 000, output is 1111
At time	10, input is 001, output is 1111
At time	13, input is 001, output is 0111
At time	20, input is 101, output is 0111
At time	23, input is 101, output is 0101
At time	26, input is 101, output is 1101
At time	30, input is 111, output is 1101
At time	33, input is 111, output is 1100
At time	36, input is 111, output is 1110
At time	40, input is 011, output is 1110
At time	44, input is 011, output is 1011
At time	50, input is 001, output is 1011
At time	54, input is 001, output is 0111

11.3.2   A Flip-flop

Here is a description of a master-slave D-type flip-flop and a testbench that exercises it.

```
module MSDFF (D, C, Q, Qbar);
  input D, C;
  output Q, Qbar;

  not
    NT1 (NotD, D),
    NT2 (NotC, C),
    NT3 (NotY, Y);
```

217

```
    nand
      ND1 (D1, D, C),
      ND2 (D2, C, NotD),
      ND3 (Y, D1, Ybar),
      ND4 (Ybar, Y, D2),
      ND5 (Y1, Y, NotC),
      ND6 (Y2, NotY, NotC),
      ND7 (Q, Qbar, Y1),
      ND8 (Qbar, Y2, Q);
  endmodule

  module Test;
    reg D, C;
    wire Q, Qb;

    MSDFF M1 (D, C, Q, Qb);

    always
      #5 C = ~C;

    initial
      begin
        D = 0;
        C = 0;
        #40 D = 1;
        #40 D = 0;
        #40 D = 1;
        #40 D = 0;
        $stop;
      end

    initial
      $monitor ("Time=%t ::", $time, " C=%b, D=%b, Q=%b,
          Qb=%b", C, D, Q, Qb);
  endmodule
```

In this testbench, a monitor is set on the two inputs and the two outputs of the flip-flop. Thus, anytime a value changes, the specified argument string is printed out. Here is the output produced upon execution.

```
Time=          0 :: C=0, D=0, Q=x, Qb=x
Time=          5 :: C=1, D=0, Q=x, Qb=x
```

```
Time=                10 :: C=0, D=0, Q=0, Qb=1
Time=                15 :: C=1, D=0, Q=0, Qb=1
Time=                20 :: C=0, D=0, Q=0, Qb=1
Time=                25 :: C=1, D=0, Q=0, Qb=1
Time=                30 :: C=0, D=0, Q=0, Qb=1
Time=                35 :: C=1, D=0, Q=0, Qb=1
Time=                40 :: C=0, D=1, Q=0, Qb=1
Time=                45 :: C=1, D=1, Q=0, Qb=1
Time=                50 :: C=0, D=1, Q=1, Qb=0
Time=                55 :: C=1, D=1, Q=1, Qb=0
Time=                60 :: C=0, D=1, Q=1, Qb=0
Time=                65 :: C=1, D=1, Q=1, Qb=0
Time=                70 :: C=0, D=1, Q=1, Qb=0
Time=                75 :: C=1, D=1, Q=1, Qb=0
Time=                80 :: C=0, D=0, Q=1, Qb=0
Time=                85 :: C=1, D=0, Q=1, Qb=0
Time=                90 :: C=0, D=0, Q=0, Qb=1
Time=                95 :: C=1, D=0, Q=0, Qb=1
Time=               100 :: C=0, D=0, Q=0, Qb=1
Time=               105 :: C=1, D=0, Q=0, Qb=1
Time=               110 :: C=0, D=0, Q=0, Qb=1
Time=               115 :: C=1, D=0, Q=0, Qb=1
Time=               120 :: C=0, D=1, Q=0, Qb=1
Time=               125 :: C=1, D=1, Q=0, Qb=1
Time=               130 :: C=0, D=1, Q=1, Qb=0
Time=               135 :: C=1, D=1, Q=1, Qb=0
Time=               140 :: C=0, D=1, Q=1, Qb=0
Time=               145 :: C=1, D=1, Q=1, Qb=0
Time=               150 :: C=0, D=1, Q=1, Qb=0
Time=               155 :: C=1, D=1, Q=1, Qb=0
```

11.4   Reading Vectors from a Text File

It is possible to read vectors (could contain stimulus and expected values) from a text file using the **$readmemb** system task. Here is such an example of testing a 3-bit full-adder circuit. Assume that file "test.vec" contains the following two vectors.

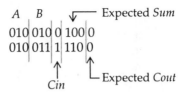

The first three bits correspond to input *A*, next three bits are for input *B*, next bit is the carry-in bit, eight to tenth bits are the expected sum result and the last bit is the expected carry-out. Here is the full-adder module and its test-bench.

```
module Adder1Bit (A, B, Cin, Sum, Cout);
  input A, B, Cin;
  output Sum, Cout;

  assign Sum = (A ^ B) ^ Cin;
  assign Cout = (A & B) | (A & Cin) | (B & Cin);
endmodule

module Adder3Bit (First, Second, Carry_In,
                  Sum_Out, Carry_Out);
  input [0:2] First, Second;
  input Carry_In;
  output [0:2] Sum_Out;
  output Carry_Out;
  wire [0:1] Car;

  Adder1Bit
    A1 (First[2], Second[2], Carry_In,
       Sum_Out[2], Car[1]),
    A2 (First[1], Second[1], Car[1], Sum_Out[1], Car[0]),
    A3 (First[0], Second[0], Car[0],
       Sum_Out[0], Carry_Out);
endmodule
```

```
module TestBench;
  parameter BITS = 11, WORDS = 2;
  reg [1:BITS] Vmem [1:WORDS];
  reg [0:2] A, B, Sum_Ex;
  reg Cin, Cout_Ex;
  integer J;
  wire [0:2] Sum;
  wire Cout;

  // Instantiate the module under test.
  Adder3Bit   F1 (A, B, Cin, Sum, Cout);

  initial
    begin
      $readmemb ("test.vec", Vmem);

      for (J = 1; J <= WORDS; J = J + 1)
        begin
          {A, B, Cin, Sum_Ex, Cout_Ex} = Vmem [J];
          #5;  // Wait for 5 time units for circuit to settle.

          if ((Sum !== Sum_Ex) || (Cout !== Cout_Ex))
            $display ("****Mismatch on vector %b *****",
                        Vmem [J]);
          else
            $display ("No mismatch on vector %b", Vmem [J]);
        end
    end
endmodule
```

A memory *Vmem* is first defined; the word size corresponds to the number of bits in each vector and the number of words in memory corresponds to the number of vectors in the file. The $**readmemb** system task reads the vectors in the file "test.vec" into the memory *Vmem*. The for-loop goes through each of the memory words, that is, each vector, applies these to the module under test, waits for the module to be stable and probes the module outputs. A conditional statement is used to compare expected output values and the monitored output values. If any mismatch occurs, a message is printed to the output. Here is the output produced when the above test bench is executed. Since there are no errors in the model, no mismatches are reported.

No mismatch on vector 01001001000
No mismatch on vector 01001111100

11.5   Writing Vectors to a Text File

In the previous section on testbench examples, we saw how values are printed to output. Values of signals in a design can be printed to a file as well by using the display system tasks that write to a file such as **$fdisplay**, **$fmonitor** and **$fstrobe**. Here is the same testbench example as is the previous section, but in this case, the testbench prints out all the input vectors and observed output vectors to a file "mon.out".

```
module F_Test_Bench;
  parameter BITS = 11, WORDS = 2;
  reg [1:BITS] Vmem [1:WORDS];
  reg [0:2] A, B, Sum_Ex;
  reg Cin, Cout_Ex;
  integer J;
  wire [0:2] Sum;
  wire Cout;

  // Instantiate the module under test.
  Adder3Bit   F1 (A, B, Cin, Sum, Cout);

  initial
    begin: INIT_LABEL
      integer Mon_Out_File;

      Mon_Out_File = $fopen ("mon.out");
      $readmemb ("test.vec", Vmem);

      for (J = 1; J <= WORDS; J = J + 1)
        begin
          {A, B, Cin, Sum_Ex, Cout_Ex} = Vmem[J];
          #5; // Wait for 5 time units for circuit to settle.

          if ((Sum !== Sum_Ex) || (Cout !== Cout_Ex))
            $display ("****Mismatch on vector %b *****",
                    Vmem[J]);
```

```
      else
        $display ("No mismatch on vector %b", Vmem[J]);

        // Write the input and output vectors to a file:
        $fdisplay (Mon_Out_File,
                "Input = %b%b%b, Output = %b%b",
                A, B, Cin, Sum, Cout);
    end

      $fclose (Mon_Out_File);
    end
endmodule
```

Here is what is contained in the file "mon.out" after simulation.

```
Input = 0100100, Output = 1000
Input = 0100111, Output = 1100
```

11.6   Some More Examples

11.6.1   A Clock Divider

A complete testbench that uses the waveform application method is shown next. The module under test is called *Div*. The output responses are written into a file for later comparison.

```
module Div (Ck, Reset, TestN, Ena);
  input Ck, Reset, TestN;
  output Ena;
  reg [0:3] Counter;

  always
    @ (posedge Ck) begin
      if (~Reset)
        Counter = 0;
      else
        begin
```

```
                if (~ TestN)
                  Counter = 15;
                else
                  Counter = Counter + 1;
            end
        end

    assign Ena = (Counter == 15) ? 1 : 0;
endmodule

module Div_TB;
    integer Out_File;
    reg Clock, Reset, TestN;
    wire Enable;

    initial
        Out_File = $fopen ("out.vec");

    always
        begin
            #5 Clock = 0;
            #3 Clock = 1;
        end

    Div D1 (Clock, Reset, TestN, Enable);

    initial
        begin
            Reset = 0;
            #50 Reset = 1;
        end

    initial
        begin
            TestN = 0;
            #100 TestN = 1;
            #50 TestN = 0;
            #50 $fclose (Out_File);
            $finish;          // Terminate simulation.
        end

    // For every event on the Enable output signal,
    // write to file.
```

```
initial
    $fmonitor (Out_File, "Enable changed to %b at time %t",
        Enable, $time);
endmodule
```

Here is the output contained in the "out.vec" file.

Enable changed to x at time	0
Enable changed to 0 at time	8
Enable changed to 1 at time	56
Enable changed to 0 at time	104
Enable changed to 1 at time	152

11.6.2   A Factorial Design

This example illustrates a different approach to stimulus generation; in this case the stimulus value is generated based on the state of the module under test. This approach is useful in testing a finite-state machine for which different input stimulus is applied based on the machine's state. Consider a design in which the objective is to compute the factorial of an input number. The handshake mechanism between the module under test and the test bench model is shown in Figure 11-9.

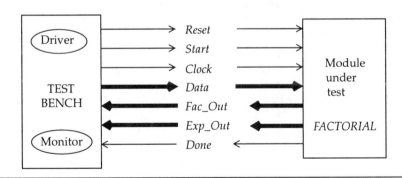

Figure 11-9   Handshake between test bench and entity under test.

The *Reset* input to the module resets the factorial model to an initial state. The *Start* signal is set after the *Data* input is applied. When computation is complete, the output *Done* is set to indicate that the computed result appears on the *Fac_Out* and *Exp_Out* outputs. The resulting factorial value is *Fac_Out* $* 2^{Exp\_Out}$. The test bench model provides input data on *Data* starting from values 1 to 20 in increments of one. It applies the data, sets the *Start* signal, waits for the *Done* signal, and then applies the next input data. Error messages are printed out if the values appearing at the output are not correct. The descriptions for the module and the test bench follows.

```
timescale 1ns / 1ns
module FACTORIAL (Reset, StartSig, Clk, Data, Done,
                  FacOut, ExpOut);
input Reset, StartSig, Clk;
input [4:0] Data;
output Done;
output [7:0] FacOut, ExpOut;

reg Stop;
reg [4:0] InLatch;
reg [7:0] Exponent, Result;
integer I;

initial Stop = 1;

always
  @ (posedge Clk) begin
    if ((StartSig == 1) && (Stop == 1) && (Reset == 1))
      begin
        Result = 1;
        Exponent = 0;
        InLatch = Data;
        Stop = 0;
      end
    else
      begin
        if ((InLatch > 1) && (Stop == 0))
          begin
            Result = Result * InLatch;
            InLatch = InLatch - 1;
          end

        if (InLatch < 1)
          Stop = 1;
```

```
        // Normalization:
        for (I = 1; I <= 5; I = I + 1)
          if (Result > 256)
            begin
              Result = Result / 2;
              Exponent = Exponent + 1;
            end
      end
  end

  assign Done = Stop;
  assign FacOut = Result;
  assign ExpOut = Exponent;
endmodule

module FAC_TB;
  parameter IN_MAX = 5, OUT_MAX = 8;
  parameter RESET_ST = 0, START_ST = 1, APPL_DATA_ST = 2,
            WAIT_RESULT_ST = 3;
  reg Clk, Reset, Start;
  wire Done;
  reg [IN_MAX-1 : 0] Data;
  wire [OUT_MAX-1 : 0] Fac_Out, Exp_Out;
  integer Next_State;
  parameter MAX_APPLY = 20;
  integer Num_Applied;

  initial
    Num_Applied = 1;

  always
    begin: CLK_P
      #6 Clk = 1;
      #4 Clk = 0;
    end

  always
    @ (negedge Clk)   // Falling edge transition.
      case (Next_State)
        RESET_ST:
          begin
            Reset = 1;
            Start = 0;
```

```
                              Next_State = APPL_DATA_ST;
                        end
                   APPL_DATA_ST:
                     begin
                       Data = Num_Applied;
                       Next_State = START_ST;
                     end
                   START_ST :
                     begin
                       Start = 1;
                       Next_State = WAIT_RESULT_ST;
                     end
                   WAIT_RESULT_ST:
                     begin
                       Reset = 0;
                       Start = 0;
                       wait (Done == 1);

                       if (Num_Applied ==
                                   Fac_Out * ('h0001 << Exp_Out))
                         $display ("Incorrect result from factorial",
                                   " model for input value %d", Data);

                       Num_Applied = Num_Applied + 1;

                       if (Num_Applied < MAX_APPLY)
                         Next_State = APPL_DATA_ST;
                       else
                         begin
                           $display ("Test completed successfully");
                           $finish;   // Terminate simulation.
                         end
                     end
                   default :
                     Next_State = START_ST;
                 endcase

     // Apply to module under test:
     FACTORIAL    F1    (Reset, Start, Clk, Data, Done,
                        Fac_Out, Exp_Out);
   endmodule
```

11.6.3   A Sequence Detector

Here is a model for a sequence detector. The model checks for a sequence of three consecutive one's on the data line. Data is checked on every falling edge of clock. Figure 11-10 shows the state diagram. Here is the model with its test bench.

```verilog
module Count3_1s (Data, Clock, Detect3_1s);
  input Data, Clock;
  output Detect3_1s;
  integer Count;
  reg Detect3_1s;

  initial
    begin
      Count = 0;
      Detect3_1s = 0;
    end

  always
    @ (negedge Clock) begin
      if (Data == 1)
        Count = Count + 1;
      else
        Count = 0;

      if (Count >= 3)
        Detect3_1s = 1;
      else
        Detect3_1s = 0;
    end
endmodule

module Top;
  reg    Data, Clock;
  integer Out_File;

  // Instantiate module under test;
  Count3_1s    F1   (Data, Clock, Detect);

  initial
    begin
```

```
        Clock = 0;

      forever
        #5  Clock = ~Clock;
    end

  initial
    begin
      Data = 0;
      #5  Data = 1;
      #40  Data = 0;
      #10  Data = 1;
      #40  Data = 0;
      #20 $stop;        // Stop simulation.
    end

  initial
    begin
      // Save monitor information in file.
      Out_File = $fopen ("results.vectors");
      $fmonitor (Out_File,
                 "Clock = %b, Data = %b, Detect = %b",
                 Clock, Data, Detect);
    end
endmodule
```

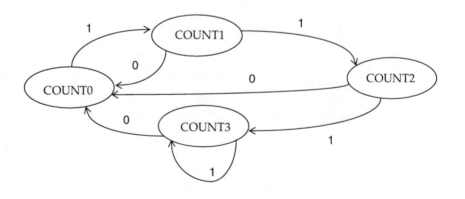

Figure 11-10   A sequence detector.

11.7   Exercises

1. Generate a clock with an on-period and an off-period of 3ns and 10ns respectively.

2. Write a Verilog HDL model that generates the waveform shown in Figure 11-11.

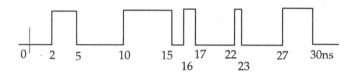

Figure 11-11 A waveform.

3. Generate a clock *ClockV* that is phase-delayed from the clock *Clk_D* described in module *Gen_Clk_D* (Figure 11-6). The phase-delay is 15ns. [Hint: Using a continuous assignment statement may not be appropriate].

4. Write a test bench that tests a sequence detector. The detector checks an input data stream on every positive clock edge for a pattern 10010. If such a pattern is found, the output is set to a 1, else it is set to a 0.

5. Write a module that generates two clocks, *ClockA* and *ClockB*. *ClockA* starts with a delay of 10ns while *ClockB* starts with a delay of 40ns. Both clocks have the same on-off period, on-period is 1ns while the off-period is 2ns. *ClockB* is synchronized with the edges of *ClockA* but has opposite polarity.

6. Describe a behavioral model for a 4-bit adder / subtracter. Exercise this model with a test bench. All input values and expected values are described within the test bench itself. Dump the input values, expected values and monitored output values to a text file.

7. Describe an ALU that performs all the relational operations (<, <=, >, >=) on two 4-bit operands. Write a test bench that reads the test patterns and the expected result from a text file.

8. Write a module that performs an arithmetic shift of an input vector. Specify the size of the input as a parameter with a default value of 32. Also specify the amount of shift as a parameter with a default value of 1. Write a test bench that tests such a module which performs an arithmetic shift on a 12-bit vector and shifts 8 times.

9. Write a model for an *N* times clock multiplier. The input is a reference clock of an unknown frequency. The output should be synchronized with every positive edge of the reference clock. [Hint: Determine the clock period of the reference clock].

10. Write a model that displays the time whenever a 0 to 1 transition occurs on an input clock.

11. Write a model for a counter that counts the number of clock pulses (positive edges) that occur during the period *Count_Flag* is 1. If count exceeds *MAX_COUNT*, the *OverFlow* output is set and counter stays at the *MAX_COUNT* limit. The rising edge of *Count_Flag* causes the counter to reset to 0 and start counting again. Write a test bench to test this model.

12. Write a model for a parameterized Gray code counter. Default it to a size of 3. The counter gets asynchronously reset when the variable *Reset* is 0. The counter transitions on every negative edge of a clock. Then instantiate a 4-bit Gray code counter in a test bench and test the model.

13. Write a behavioral model for an asynchronous reset toggle flip-flop. If toggle is 1, the output toggles between 0 and 1. If toggle is 0, output stays in previous state. Then, using the specify block, specify a setup time of 2ns and a hold time of 3ns. Verify the model using a test bench.

❑

Chapter 12

MODELING EXAMPLES

This chapter provides a number of hardware modeling examples using Verilog HDL.

12.1 Modeling Simple Elements

A basic hardware element is a wire. A wire can be modeled in Verilog HDL as a net data type. Consider a 4-bit and gate, the behavior of which is described next.

```
`timescale 1ns / 1ns
module And4 (A, B, C);
  input [3:0] B, C;
  output [3:0] A;

  assign #5 A = B & C;
endmodule
```

The delay for the & (and) logic is specified to be 5ns. The hardware represented by this model is shown in Figure 12-1.

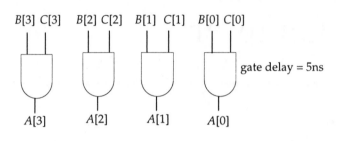

Figure 12-1 A 4-bit and gate.

This example and the one following show that Boolean equations can be modeled as expressions in continuous assignment statements. Wires can be modeled as net data types. For example, in the following description, *F* represents a wire that connects the output of the ~ (not) operator to the input of the ^ (xor) operator. Figure 12-2 shows the circuit represented by the module.

```
module Boolean_Ex (D, G, E);
    input G, E;
    output D;
    wire F;

    assign F = ~ E;
    assign D = F ^ G;
endmodule
```

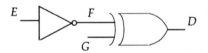

Figure 12-2 A combinational circuit.

Consider the following behavior and its corresponding hardware representation as shown in Figure 12-3.

```
module Asynchronous;
  wire A, B, C, D;

  assign C = A | D;
  assign A = ~ (B & C);
endmodule
```

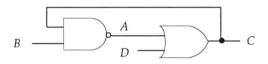

Figure 12-3   An asynchronous loop.

This circuit has an asynchronous loop. If the model were simulated with a certain set of values ($B = 1$, $D = 0$), simulation time would never advance because the simulator would always be iterating between the two assignments. The iteration time would be two zero delays. Therefore, extra caution must be exercised when values are assigned to nets using continuous assignment that have zero delay and when these same net values are used in expressions.

In certain cases, it is desirable to have such an asynchronous loop. An example of such an asynchronous loop is shown next; the statement represents a periodic waveform with a cycle of 20ns. Its hardware representation is shown in Figure 12-4. Note that such an always statement needs an initial statement that initializes the register to either a 0 or a 1, else the register will be stuck at the value **x**.

```
reg Ace;

initial
  Ace = 0;

always
  #10 Ace = ~ Ace;
```

Elements of a vector net or a register can be accessed, as either a single element called bit-select, or a slice called part-select. For example,

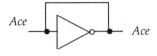

Figure 12-4 A clock generator.

```
reg A;
reg [0:4] C;
reg [5:0] B, D;

always
  begin
    . . .
    D[4:0] = B[5:1] | C;
            // D[4:0] and B[5:1] are part-selects.
    D[5] = A & B[5];    // D[5] and B[5] are bit-selects.
  end
```

The first procedural assignment implies:

```
D[4] = B[5] | C[0];
D[3] = B[4] | C[1];
. . .
```

Bit-selects, part-selects and vectors can be concatenated to form larger vectors. For example,

```
wire [7:0] C, CC;
wire CX;
. . .
assign C = {CX, CC[6:0]};
```

It is also possible to refer to an element of a vector whose index value is computable only at runtime. For example,

```
Adf = Plb [K];
```

implies a decoder whose output is *Adf*, and *K* specifies the selection address. *Plb* is a vector; it models the behavior of the decoder.

Shift operations can be performed using the predefined shift operators. Alternately, shift operations can be modeled using the concatenation operator. For example,

```
wire [0:7] A, Z;
. . .
assign Z = {A[1:7], A[0]}; // A left-rotate operation.
assign Z = {A[7], A[0:6]}; // A right-rotate operation.
assign Z = {A[1:7], 1'b0}; // A left-shift operation.
```

Subfields of a vector, called part-select, can also be used in expressions. For example, consider a 32-bit instruction register, *Instr_Reg*, in which the first 16 bits denote the address, next 8 bits represent the opcode, and the remaining 8 bits represent the index. Given the following declarations,

```
reg [31:0] Memory [0:1023];
wire [31:0] Instr_Reg;
wire [15:0] Address;
wire [7:0] Op_Code, Index;
wire [0:9] Prog_Ctr;
wire Read_Ctl;
```

one way to read the subfield information from the *Instr_Reg* is to use three continuous assignment statements. The part-selects of the instruction register are assigned to specific wires.

```
assign Instr_Reg = Memory [Prog_Ctr];

assign Address = Instr_Reg[31:16];
assign Op_Code = Instr_Reg[15:8];
assign Index = Instr_Reg[7:0];
. . .
always
  @(posedge Read_Ctl)
    Task_Call (Address, Op_Code, Index);
```

A tristate gate can be modeled behaviorally using a continuous assignment statement. An example is:

```
wire TriOut = Enable ? TriIn : 1'bz;
```

When *Enable* is 1, *TriOut* gets the value of *TriIn*. When *Enable* is 0, *TriOut* has a high impedance value.

12.2   Different Styles of Modeling

This section gives examples of the three different modeling styles provided by the language: dataflow, behavioral, and structural. Consider the circuit shown in Figure 12-5, which saves the value of the input *A* into a register and then multiplies it with input *C*.

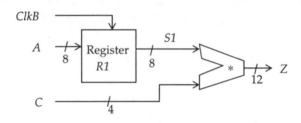

Figure 12-5   A buffered multiplier.

The first modeling style is the dataflow style in which continuous assignment statements are used to model the circuit.

```
module Save_Mult_Df (A, C, ClkB, Z);
  input [0:7] A;
  input [0:3] C;
  input ClkB;
  output [0:11] Z;
  wire S1;

  assign Z = S1 * C;
  assign S1 = ClkB ? A : S1;
endmodule
```

This representation does not directly imply any structure, but implicitly describes it. However, its functionality is very clear. The register has been modeled using a clock control.

The second way to describe the circuit is to model it as a sequential program using an always statement with a sequential block.

```
module Save_Mult_Seq (A, C, ClkB, Z);
  input [0:7] A;
  input [0:3] C;
  input ClkB;
  output [0:11] Z;
  reg [0:11] Z;

  always
    @(A or C or ClkB)
      begin: SEQ
        // The block is labeled so that a local register S1
        // can be declared.
        reg [0:7] S1;

        if (ClkB)
          S1 = A;

        Z = S1 * C;
      end
endmodule
```

This model also describes the behavior, but does not imply any structure, either explicitly or implicitly. In this case, the register has been modeled using an if statement.

The third way to describe the *Save_Mult* circuit is to model it as a netlist assuming the existence of an 8-bit register and an 8-bit multiplier.

```
module Save_Mult_Netlist (A, C, ClkB, Z);
  input [0:7] A;
  input [0:3] C;
  input ClkB;
  output [0:11] Z;
  wire [0:7] S1, S3;
  wire [0:15] S2;
```

```
Reg8    R1 (.Din(A), .Clk(ClkB), .Dout(S1));
Mult8   M1 (.A(S1), .B({4'b0000, C}), .Z(Z));
endmodule
```

This description explicitly describes the structure, but the behavior is unknown. This is because the *Reg8* and *Mult8* module names are arbitrary, and they could have any behavior associated with them.

Of these three different modeling styles, the behavioral style of modeling is generally the fastest to simulate.

12.3   Modeling Delays

Consider a 3-input nor gate. Its behavior can be modeled using a continuous assignment, such as shown in the following example.

```
assign #12 Gate_Out = ~ (A | B | C);
```

This statement models the nor gate with a delay of 12 time units. This delay represents the time from an event on signal A, B, or C until the result value appears on signal *Gate_Out*. An event could be any value change, for example, x -> z, x -> 0, or 1 -> 0.

If the rise time and the fall time were to be explicitly modeled, use two delays in the assignment, such as:

```
assign #(12, 14) Zoom = ~ (A | B | C);
/* 12 is the rise delay, 14 is the fall delay and
   min(12, 14) = 12 is the transition to x delay */
```

In case of logic that can be assigned the value z, a third delay value, which is the turn-off delay, can also be specified, such as:

```
assign #(12, 14, 10) Zoom = A > B ? C : 'bz;
// Rise delay is 12, fall delay is 14, transition to x delay
// is min(12, 14, 10), and turn-off delay is 10.
```

Each of the delay values can also be represented using *min:typ:max* notation, such as in the following example.

```
assign #(9:10:11, 11:12:13, 13:14:15) Zoom = A > B ? C : 'bz;
```

A delay value could in general be an expression.

Delays in primitive gate instances and UDPs can be modeled by specifying the delay values in the instantiation. Here is an example of a 5-input primitive and gate.

```
and #(2, 3) A1 (Ot, In1, In2, In3, In4, In5);
```

The output rise delay has been specified as 2 time units and the output fall delay has been specified as 3 time units.

Delays in a module at port boundaries can be specified using a specify block. For example, here is an example of a half-adder module.

```
module Half_Adder (A, B, S, C);
  input A, B;
  output S, C;

specify
  (A => S) = (1.2, 0.8);
  (B => S) = (1.0, 0.6);
  (A => C) = (1.2, 1.0);
  (B => C) = (1.2, 0.6);
endspecify

  assign S = A ^ B;
  assign C = A | B;
endmodule
```

Instead of modeling the delays in the continuous assignments, the delays have been modeled using a specify block. Is there a way to specify the delays external to the module? One option is to use the SDF[1] (Standard Delay Format) and the backannotation mechanism possibly provided by a Verilog simulator. If this information needs to be specified in the Verilog HDL model explicitly,

---

1. See Bibliography.

one approach is to create two dummy modules on top of the *Half_Adder* module each with a different set of delays.

```verilog
module Half_Adder (A, B, S, C);
  input A, B;
  output S, C;

  assign S = A ^ B;
  assign C = A | B;
endmodule

module Ha_Opt (A, B, S, C);
  input A, B;
  output S, C;

  specify
    (A => S) = (1.2, 0.8);
    (B => S) = (1.0, 0.6);
    (A => C) = (1.2, 1.0);
    (B => C) = (1.2, 0.6);
  endspecify

  Half_Adder    H1 (A, B, S, C);
endmodule

module Ha_Pess (A, B, S, C);
  input A, B;
  output S, C;

  specify
    (A => S) = (0.6, 0.4);
    (B => S) = (0.5, 0.3);
    (A => C) = (0.6, 0.5);
    (B => C) = (0.6, 0.3);
  endspecify

  Half_Adder    H2 (A, B, S, C);
endmodule
```

With these modules, the module *Half_Adder* is independent of any delays, and depending on which delay mode that you would like to use, simulate the appropriate top-level module *Ha_Opt* or *Ha_Pess*.

Transport Delays

Delays specified in continuous assignments and gate-level primitives model inertial delay. Transport delay can be modeled using a non-blocking assignment with an intra-statement delay. Here is an example.

```
module Transport (WaveA, DelayedWave);
  parameter TRANSPORT_DELAY = 500;
  input WaveA;
  output DelayedWave;
  reg DelayedWave;

  always
    @(WaveA) DelayedWave <= #TRANSPORT_DELAY WaveA;
endmodule
```

The always statement contains a non-blocking assignment with an intra-statement delay. Any change on *WaveA* gets scheduled on *DelayedWave* *TRANSPORT_DELAY* in the future. Consequently, a waveform that appears on *WaveA* appears on *DelayedWave* delayed by *TRANSPORT_DELAY*; an example of such a delayed waveform is shown in Figure 12-6.

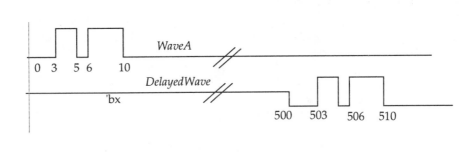

Figure 12-6 Transport delay example.

12.4   Modeling Conditional Operations

Operations that occur under certain conditions can be modeled using either a continuous assignment with a conditional operator, or using an `if` statement or a case statement in an always statement. Let us consider an arithmetic logic circuit. Its behavior can be modeled using a continuous assignment as shown below.

```
module Simple_ALU (A, B, C, PM, ALU);
  input [0:3] A, B, C;
  input PM;
  output [0:3] ALU;

  assign ALU = PM ? A + B : A - B;
endmodule
```

A multiplexer can also be modeled using an always statement. The value of the select lines are first determined and, based on this value, a case statement selects the appropriate input that is to be assigned to the output.

```
`timescale 1ns / 1ns
module Multiplexer (Sel, A, B, C, D, Mux_Out);
  input [0:1] Sel;
  input A, B, C, D;
  output Mux_Out;
  reg Mux_Out;
  reg Temp;
  parameter MUX_DELAY = 15;

  always
    @ (Sel or A or B or C or D)
      begin: P1
        case (Sel)
          0: Temp = A;
          1: Temp = B;
          2: Temp = C;
          3: Temp = D;
        endcase
```

```
        Mux_Out = #MUX_DELAY Temp;
      end
    endmodule
```

The multiplexer could also have been modeled using a continuous assignment of the form:

```
assign #MUX_DELAY Mux_Out = (Sel == 0) ? A : (Sel == 1) ? B :
                           (Sel == 2) ? C : (Sel == 3) ? D : 1'bx;
```

12.5   Modeling Synchronous Logic

So far in this chapter, most of the examples that we have seen are combinational logic. For modeling synchronous logic, the register data type has been provided in the language to model registers and memories. However not every register data type infers synchronous logic. A common way to model synchronous logic is by controlling the assignment.

Consider the following example, which shows how controlling a register can model a synchronous edge-triggered D-type flip-flop.

```
`timescale 1ns / 1ns
module D_Flip_Flop (D, Clock, Q);
  input D, Clock;
  output Q;
  reg Q;

  always
    @(posedge Clock)
      Q = #5 D;
endmodule
```

The semantics of the always statement indicates that when there is a rising edge on *Clock*, *Q* will get the value of *D* after 5ns, else the value of *Q* does not change (a register retains its value until it is assigned a new value). The behavior in the always statement expresses the semantics of a D-type flip-flop. Given this module, an 8-bit register can be modeled as follows.

```
module Register8 (D, Q, Clock);
  parameter START = 0, STOP = 7;
  input [START : STOP] D;
  input Clock;
  output [START : STOP] Q;
  wire [START : STOP] Cak;

  D_Flip_Flop   DFF0
            [START : STOP]  (.D(D), .Clock (Cak), .Q(Q));

  buf   B1   (Cak[0], Cak[1], Cak[2], Cak[3], Cak[4],
             Cak[5], Cak[6], Cak[7], Clock);
endmodule
```

Consider a gated cross-coupled latch circuit, as shown in Figure 12-7, and its dataflow model.

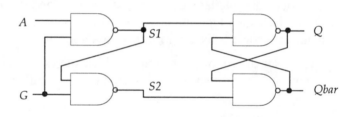

Figure 12-7 A gated latch.

```
module Gated_FF (A, G, Q, Qbar);
  input A, G;
  output Q, Qbar;
  wire S1, S2;

  assign S1 = ~ (A & G);
  assign S2 = ~ (S1 & G);
  assign Q = ~ (Qbar & S1);
  assign Qbar = ~ (Q & S2);
endmodule
```

In this example, the semantics of the continuous assignments implies a latch.

A memory can be modeled as an array of registers. Here is an example. *ASIZE* is the number of bits on the address port, and *DSIZE* is the number of bits on the data port of the RAM.

```
module RAM_Generic (Address, Data_In, Data_Out, RW);
  parameter ASIZE = 6, DSIZE = 4;
  input [ASIZE-1 : 0] Address;
  input [DSIZE-1 : 0] Data_In;
  input RW;
  output [DSIZE-1 : 0] Data_Out;
  reg [DSIZE-1 : 0] Data_Out;
  reg [0 : DSIZE-1] Mem_FF [0 : 63];

  always
    @ (RW)
      if (RW)            // Read
        Data_Out = Mem_FF [Address];
      else
        Mem_FF [Address] = Data_In;
endmodule
```

Synchronous logic can also be modeled using level-sensitive or edge-triggered controls. For example, a level-sensitive D flip-flop can be modeled as follows.

```
module Level_Sens_FF (Strobe, D, Q, Qbar);
  input Strobe, D;
  output Q, Qbar;
  reg Q, Qbar;

  always
    begin
      wait (Strobe == 1);
      Q = D;
      Qbar = ~D;
    end
endmodule
```

When *Strobe* is 1, any events on *D* are transferred to *Q*, but when *Strobe* becomes 0, the values in *Q* and *Qbar* are retained, and any change in input *D* no longer affects the values of *Q* and *Qbar*.

It is important to understand the semantics of a procedural assignment to determine the inference of synchronous logic. Consider the difference between the following two modules, *Body1* and *Body2*.

```
module Body1;
  reg A;

  initial A = 0;

  always A = ~A;
endmodule

module Body2;
  wire Clock;
  reg A;

  initial A = 0;

  always
    @ (Clock)
      if (~ Clock)
        A = ~ A;
endmodule
```

Module *Body1* implies the circuit shown in Figure 12-8, while module *Body2* implies the circuit shown in Figure 12-9.

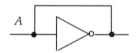

Figure 12-8   No flip-flop implied.

If *Body1* were simulated as is, simulation would go into an endless loop due to the zero delay asynchronous loop (simulation time does not advance). In module *Body2*, the value of *A* is latched only on the falling edge of the *Clock* signal, and thereafter, any changes on *A* (input of flip-flop) do not affect the output of flip-flop.

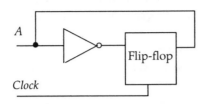

Figure 12-9 A flip-flop implied.

12.6   A Generic Shift Register

A generic serial-in, serial-out shift register can be modeled using a for-loop with an always statement. The number of registers is specified as a parameter so that it can be modified when the generic shift register is instantiated in another design.

```
module Shift_Reg (D, Clock, Z);
  input D, Clock;
  output Z;
  parameter NUM_REG = 6;
  reg [1 : NUM_REG] Q;
  integer P;

  always
    @ (negedge Clock) begin
      // Shift register one bit right:
      for (P = 1; P < NUM_REG; P = P + 1)
        Q[P+1] = Q[P];

      // Push in the serial data:
      Q[1] = D;
    end

  // Get the output from the rightmost register:
  assign Z = Q[NUM_REG];
endmodule
```

Shift registers of varying sizes can be obtained by instantiating module *ShiftReg* using different parameter values.

```
module Dummy;
  wire Data, Clk, Za, Zb, Zc;

  // 6-bit shift register:
  Shift_Reg SRA (Data, Clk, Za);

  // 4-bit shift register:
  Shift_Reg #4 SRB (Data, Clk, Zb);

  // 10-bit shift register:
  Shift_Reg #10 SRC (Data, Clk, Zc);
endmodule
```

12.7   State Machine Modeling

State machines can usually be modeled using a case statement with an always statement. The state information is stored in a register. The multiple branches of the case statement contain the behavior for each state. Here is an example of a simple multiplication algorithm represented as a state machine. When the *Reset* signal is high, the accumulator *Acc* and the counter *Count* are initialized. When *Reset* goes low, multiplication starts. If the bit of the multiplier *Mplr* in position *Count* is 1, the multiplicand *Mcnd* is added to the accumulator. Next, the multiplicand is left-shifted by one bit, and the counter is incremented. If *Count* is 16, multiplication is complete and the *Done* signal is set high. If not, the *Count* bit of the multiplier *Mplr* is checked and the always statement repeated. The state diagram is shown in Figure 12-10 and the corresponding state machine model is shown next.

```
module Multiply (Mplr, Mcnd, Clock, Reset, Done, Acc);
      // Mplr is multiplier, Mcnd is multiplicand.
  input [15:0] Mplr, Mcnd;
  input Clock, Reset;
  output Done;
  reg Done;
  output [31:0] Acc;
  reg [31:0] Acc;
```

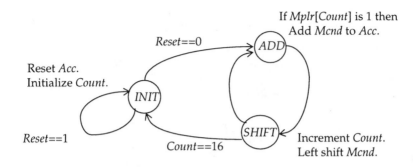

Figure 12-10   State diagram for multiplier.

```
parameter INIT = 0, ADD = 1, SHIFT = 2;
reg [0:1] Mpy_State;
reg [31:0] Mcnd_Temp;

initial Mpy_State = INIT;    // Initial state is INIT.

always
  @(negedge Clock) begin: PROCESS
    integer Count;

  case (Mpy_State)
    INIT :
      if (Reset)
        Mpy_State = INIT;
        /* The above statement is not really necessary
           since Mpy_State will retain its old value */
      else
        begin
          Acc = 0;
          Count = 0;
          Mpy_State = ADD;
          Done = 0;
          Mcnd_Temp[15:0] = Mcnd;
          Mcnd_Temp[31:16] = 16'd0;
        end

    ADD :
      begin
        if (Mplr[Count])
```

```
                    Acc = Acc + Mcnd_Temp;

              Mpy_State = SHIFT;
          end

      SHIFT :
        begin
          // Left-shift Mcnd_Temp:
          Mcnd_Temp = {Mcnd_Temp[30:0], 1'b0};
          Count = Count + 1;

          if (Count == 16)
            begin
              Mpy_State = INIT;
              Done = 1;
            end
          else
            Mpy_State = ADD;
        end
      endcase          // case Mpy_State
    end                // sequential block PROCESS
  endmodule
```

The register *Mpy_State* holds the state of the model. Initially, the model is in state *INIT* and it stays in this state as long as *Reset* is true. When *Reset* is false, the accumulator *Acc* is cleared, the counter *Count* is reset, the multiplicand *Mcnd* is loaded into a temporary variable *Mcnd_Temp*, and the model advances to state *ADD*. When model is in the *ADD* state, the multiplicand in *Mcnd_Temp* is added to *Acc* only if the bit at the *Count* position of the multiplier is a 1 and then the model advances to state *SHIFT*. In this state, the multiplier is left-shifted once, the counter is incremented, and if the counter value is 16, *Done* is set to true and the model returns to state *INIT*. At this time, *Acc* contains the result of the multiplication. If the counter value was less than 16, the model repeats itself going through states *ADD* and *SHIFT* until the counter value becomes 16.

State transitions occur at every falling edge of the clock; this is specified using the @(**negedge** *Clock*) timing control.

12.8   Interacting State Machines

Interacting state machines can be described as separate always statements communicating via common registers. Consider the state diagram shown in Figure 12-11 for two interacting processes, *TX*, a transmitter, and *MP*, a microprocessor. If process *TX* is not busy, process *MP* sets the data to be transmitted on a data bus and sends a signal *Load_TX* to process *TX* to load the data and begin transmitting. *TX_Busy* is set by process *TX* during transmission to indicate that it is busy and cannot receive any further data from process *MP*.

A skeleton model for these two interacting processes is shown. Only the control signals and state transitions are shown. Data manipulation code is not described.

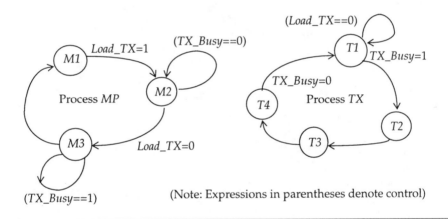

Figure 12-11   State diagram of two interacting processes.

```
module Interacting_FSM (Clock);
  input Clock;

  parameter M1 = 0, M2 = 1, M3 = 2;
  parameter T1 =0, T2 = 1, T3 = 2, T4 = 3;
  reg [0:1] MP_State;
  reg [0:1] TX_State;
  reg Load_TX, TX_Busy;
```

```verilog
always
  @(negedge Clock) begin: MP
    case (MP_State)
      M1 :         // Load data on data bus.
        begin
          Load_TX = 1;
          MP_State = M2;
        end

      M2 :      // Wait for acknowledgment.
        if (TX_Busy)
          begin
            MP_State = M3;
            Load_TX = 0;
          end

      M3 :      // Wait for TX to finish.
        if (~TX_Busy)
          MP_State = M1;
    endcase
end             // End of sequential block MP

always
  @ (negedge Clock) begin: TX
    case (TX_State)
      T1 :                    // Wait for data to load.
        if (Load_TX)
          begin
            TX_State = T2;
            TX_Busy = 1;      // Read data from data bus.
          end

      T2 :                    // Sending leading flag.
        TX_State = T3;

      T3 :
        TX_State = T4;        // Transmitting data.

      T4 :    // Sending trailing flag to end transmission.
        begin
          TX_Busy = 0;
          TX_State = T1;
        end
```

```
        endcase
    end                 // End of sequential block TX.
endmodule
```

The sequence of actions for this interacting finite-state machine is shown in Figure 12-12.

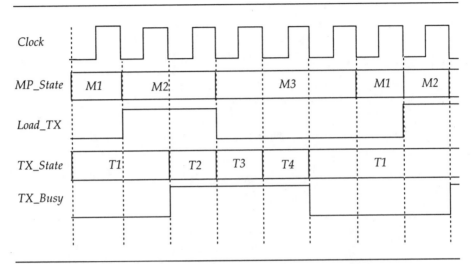

Figure 12-12 Sequence of actions for the two interacting processes.

Consider another example of two interacting processes, *DIV*, a clock divider, and *RX*, a receiver. In this case, process *DIV* generates a new clock and process *RX* goes through its sequence of states synchronized to this new clock. The state diagram is shown in Figure 12-13.

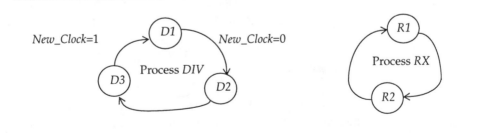

Figure 12-13 *DIV* generates clock for *RX*.

```
module Another_Example_FSM2 (Clock);
  input Clock;

  parameter D1 = 1, D2 = 2, D3 = 3;
  parameter R1 = 1, R2 = 2;
  reg [0:1] Div_State, RX_State;
  reg New_Clock;

  always
    @(posedge Clock) begin: DIV
      case (Div_State)
        D1 :
          begin
            Div_State = D2;
            New_Clock = 0;
          end

        D2 :
          Div_State = D3;

        D3 :
          begin
            New_Clock = 1;
            Div_State = D1;
          end
      endcase
    end             // Sequential block DIV

  always
    @(negedge New_Clock) begin: RX
      case (RX_State)
        R1 : RX_State = R2;
        R2 : RX_State = R1;
      endcase
    end             // Sequential block RX
endmodule
```

Sequential block *DIV* generates a new clock *New_Clock* as it goes through its sequence of states. The state transitions in this process occur on the rising edge of *Clock*. Sequential block *RX* is executed every time a falling edge on *New_Clock* occurs. The sequence of waveforms for these interacting state machines is shown in Figure 12-14.

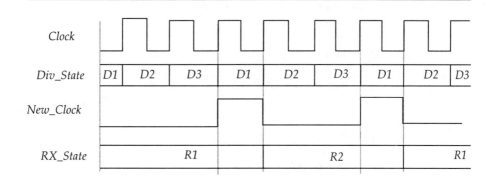

Figure 12-14   Interaction between processes *RX* and *DIV*.

12.9   Modeling a Moore FSM

The output of a Moore finite state machine (FSM) depends only on the state and not on its inputs. This type of behavior can be modeled using an always statement with a case statement that switches on the state value. An example of a state transition diagram for a Moore finite state machine is shown in Figure 12-15 and its corresponding behavior model appears next.

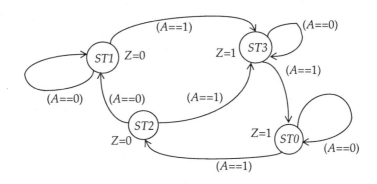

Figure 12-15   State diagram of a Moore machine.

```
module Moore_FSM (A, Clock, Z);
  input A, Clock;
  output Z;
  reg Z;

  parameter ST0 = 0, ST1 = 1, ST2 = 2, ST3 = 3;
  reg [0:1] Moore_State;

  always
    @(negedge Clock)
      case (Moore_State)
        ST0:
          begin
            Z = 1;
            if (A)
              Moore_State = ST2;
          end

        ST1 :
          begin
            Z = 0;
            if (A)
              Moore_State = ST3;
          end

        ST2:
          begin
            Z = 0;
            if (~A)
              Moore_State = ST1;
            else
              Moore_State = ST3;
          end

        ST3:
          begin
            Z = 1;
            if (A)
              Moore_State = ST0;
          end
      endcase
endmodule
```

12.10   Modeling a Mealy FSM

In a Mealy finite state machine, the outputs not only depend on the state of the machine but also on its inputs. This type of finite state machine can be modeled in a style similar to that of the Moore FSM, that is, using a single always statement. To show the variety of the language, a different style is used to model a Mealy machine. In this case we use two always statements, one that models the synchronous aspect of the finite state machine and one that models the combinational part of the finite state machine. Here is an example of a state transition table shown in Figure 12-16 and its corresponding behavior model.

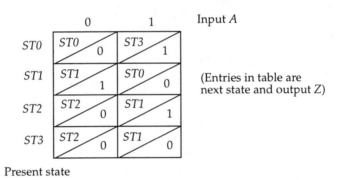

Figure 12-16   State transition table for a Mealy machine.

```
module Mealy_FSM (A, Clock, Z);
  input A, Clock;
  output Z;
  reg Z;

  parameter ST0 = 0, ST1 = 1, ST2 = 2, ST3 = 3;
  reg [1:2] P_State, N_State;

  always
    @(negedge Clock)    // Synchronous part.
      P_State = N_State;
```

```
always
  @(P_State or A) begin: COMB_PART
    case (P_State)
      ST0:
        if (A)
          begin
            Z = 1;
            N_State = ST3;
          end
        else
          Z = 0;


      ST1 :
        if (A)
          begin
            Z = 0;
            N_State = ST0;
          end
        else
          Z = 1;


      ST2 :
        if (~A)
          Z = 0;
        else
          begin
            Z = 1;
            N_State = ST1;
          end


      ST3 :
        begin
          Z = 0;
          if (~A)
            N_State = ST2;
          else
            N_State = ST1;
        end
    endcase
  end              // Sequential block COMB_PART
endmodule
```

In this type of finite state machine, it is important to put the input signals in the event list for the combinational part sequential block since the outputs may directly depend on the inputs independent of the clock. Such a condition does not occur in a Moore finite state machine since outputs depend only on states and state changes occur synchronously on clock.

12.11 A Simplified Blackjack Program

This section presents a state machine description of a simplified blackjack program. The blackjack program is played with a deck of cards. Cards 2 to 10 have values equal to their face value, and an ace has a value of either 1 or 11. The object of the game is to accept a number of random cards such that the total score (sum of values of all cards) is as close as possible to 21 without exceeding 21.

When a new card is inserted, *Card_Rdy* is true and *Card_Value* has the value of the card. *Request_Card* indicates when the program is ready to accept a new card. If a sequence of cards is accepted such that the total exceeds 21, *Lost* is set to true indicating that it has lost; otherwise *Won* is set to true indicating that the game has been won. The state sequencing is controlled by *Clock*. The input and outputs of the blackjack program are shown in Figure 12-17.

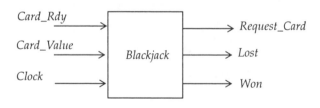

Figure 12-17 External view of blackjack program.

The behavior of the program is described in the following module declaration. The program accepts cards until its score is at least 17. The first ace is counted as a 11 unless the score exceeds 21, in which case 10 is subtracted so that the value of 1 is used for an ace. Three registers are used to store the values of the program: *Total* to hold the sum, *Current_Card_Value* to hold the value of the card read (which could be 1 through 10), and *Ace_As_11* to remember whether an ace was counted as a 11 instead of a 1. The state of the blackjack program is stored in register *BJ_State*.

```verilog
module Blackjack (Card_Rdy, Card_Value,
                       Request_Card, Won, Lost, Clock);
  input Card_Rdy, Clock;
  input [0:3] Card_Value;
  output Request_Card, Lost, Won;
  reg Request_Card, Lost, Won;

  parameter INITIAL_ST = 0, GETCARD_ST = 1,
            REMCARD_ST = 2, ADD_ST = 3, CHECK_ST = 4,
            WIN_ST = 5, BACKUP_ST = 6, LOSE_ST = 7;
  reg [0:2] BJ_State;
  reg [0:3] Current_Card_Value;
  reg [0:4] Total;
  reg Ace_As_11;

  always
    @(negedge Clock)
      case (BJ_State)
        INITIAL_ST :
          begin
            Total = 0;
            Ace_As_11 = 0;
            Won = 0;
            Lost = 0;
            BJ_State = GETCARD_ST;
          end

        GETCARD_ST :
          begin
            Request_Card = 1;

            if (Card_Rdy)
              begin
                Current_Card_Value = Card_Value;
                BJ_State = REMCARD_ST;
              end          // Else stay in GETCARD_ST state.
          end
```

```
REMCARD_ST :        // Wait for card to be removed.
  if (Card_Rdy)
    Request_Card = 0;
  else
    BJ_State = ADD_ST;

ADD_ST :
  begin
    if (~Ace_As_11 && Current_Card_Value)
      begin
        Current_Card_Value = 11;
        Ace_As_11 = 1;
      end

    Total = Total + Current_Card_Value;
    BJ_State = CHECK_ST;
  end

CHECK_ST :
  if (Total < 17)
    BJ_State = GETCARD_ST;
  else
    begin
      if (Total < 22)
        BJ_State = WIN_ST;
      else
        BJ_State = BACKUP_ST;
    end

BACKUP_ST :
  if (Ace_As_11)
    begin
      Total = Total - 10;
      Ace_As_11 = 0;
      BJ_State = CHECK_ST;
    end
  else
    BJ_State = LOSE_ST;

LOSE_ST :
  begin
    Lost = 1;
    Request_Card = 1;
```

```
        if (Card_Rdy)
          BJ_State = INITIAL_ST;
        // Else stay in this state.
      end

    WIN_ST :
      begin
        Won = 1;
        Request_Card = 1;

        if (Card_Rdy)
          BJ_State = INITIAL_ST;
        // Else stay in this state.
      end
    endcase
endmodule     // Blackjack
```

12.12 Exercises

1. Write a Verilog HDL model for a mango juice drink machine. The machine dispenses a can of mango juice that costs 15 cents. Only nickels and dimes are accepted. Any change must be returned. Test the model using a test bench.

2. Write a model that describes the behavior of a flip-flop with synchronous preset and clear.

3. Write a model for a 4-bit shift register with serial-in data, parallel-in data, a clock and parallel-out data. Test the model using a test bench.

4. Describe a D-type flip-flop using behavioral constructs. Then using this module, write a model for a 8-bit register.

5. Write a test bench that tests the blackjack model described in Section 12.11.

6. Using the shift operator, describe a decoder module and then test it with a test bench. The number of inputs to the decoder is specified as:

```
`define NUM_INPUTS 4
```
[Hint: Use the shift operator to figure out the number of outputs of decoder]

7. Write a model for a 8-bit parallel to serial converter. The input is a 8-bit vector. Send the bits out, one bit at a time, starting from the most significant bit on the rising edge of a clock. Read the next input only after all the bits of the previous input vector have been sent out.

8. Write a model for a 8-bit serial to parallel converter that does the opposite of Exercise 7. Sample the input stream after a small delay from the positive edge of clock to account for transmission delay. Connect the models written in this exercise and the one in Exercise 7 using a top level module and test it out using a test bench.

9. Write a model for a N-bit counter with a hold control. If the hold is a 1, the counter holds its value, when hold goes to 0, the counter is reset to 0 and starts counting again. Write a test bench to test this model.

10. Write a model for a generic queue, size of word in queue is N and number of words in queue in M. *InputData* is the word that gets written into the queue; the word is added to the queue when input *AddWord* is a 1. A word that is read from the queue is stored in *OutputData*; the word is read from the queue when input *ReadWord* is a 1. Flags *Empty* and *Full* are set appropriately. All transactions occur at the falling edge of clock *ClockA*. Write a test bench to test out the model.

11. Write a model for a parameterizable clock divider. The period of the output clock is $2*N$ times that of the input clock. The output clock is synchronized to the rising edge of the input clock. Write a test bench and test the model.

❑

Appendix A

SYNTAX REFERENCE

This appendix presents the complete syntax[1] of the Verilog HDL language.

A.1 Keywords

Following are the keywords of the Verilog HDL language. Note that only lower case names are keywords.

always	**and**	**assign**	
begin	**buf**	**bufif0**	**bufif1**
case	**casex**	**casez**	**cmos**
deassign	**default**	**defparam**	**disable**

---

1. Reprinted here from IEEE Std 1364-1995, Copyright © 1995, IEEE, All rights reserved.

edge	else	end	endcase	endmodule
endfunction	endprimitive	endspecify	endtable	endtask
event				

for	force	forever	fork	function

highz0	highz1

if	ifnone	initial	inout	input
integer				

join

large

macromodule	medium	module

nand	negedge	nmos	nor	not
notif0	notif1			

or	output

parameter	pmos	posedge	primitive	pull0
pull1	pullup	pulldown		

rcmos	real	realtime	reg	release
repeat	rnmos	rpmos	rtran	rtranif0
rtranif1				

scalared	small	specify	specparam	strong0
strong1	supply0	supply1		

table	task	time	tran	tranif0
tranif1	tri	tri0	tri1	triand
trior	trireg			

vectored

wait	wand	weak0	weak1	while
wire	wor			

xnor	xor

A.2   Syntax Conventions

The following conventions are used in describing the syntax, which is described using the Backus-Naur Form (BNF).

i. The syntax rules are organized in an alphabetical order by their left-hand nonterminal name.

ii. Reserved words, operators and punctuation marks that are part of the syntax appear in **boldface**.

iii. A name in *italics* prefixed to a nonterminal name represents the semantic meaning associated with that nonterminal name.

iv. The vertical bar symbol, non-bold, (|) separates alternative items.

v. Square brackets, non-bold, ([. . .]) denote optional items.

vi. Curly braces, non-bold, ({ . . . }) identify an item that is repeated zero or more times.

vii. Square brackets, parentheses, and curly braces and other characters (such as **, ;**) appearing in bold (**[** ... **]**, **(** ... **)**, **{** ... **}**) indicate characters that are part of the syntax.

viii. The starting nonterminal name is "source_text".

ix. The terminal names used in this grammar appear in upper case.

A.3   The Syntax

always_construct ::=
    always
      statement

binary_base ::=
    'b | **'B**

binary_digit ::=
    x | **X** | **z** | **Z** | **0** | **1**

binary_number ::=
    [size] binary_base binary_digit { **_** | binary_digit }

binary_operator ::=
      + | **-** | ***** | **/** | **%**
    | **==** | **!=** | **===** | **!==** | **&&** | **||** | **<** | **<=** | **>** | **>=**
    | **&** | **|** | **^** | **^~** | **~^** | **>>** | **<<**

block_item_declaration ::=
      parameter_declaration
    | reg_declaration
    | integer_declaration
    | real_declaration
    | time_declaration
    | realtime_declaration
    | event_declaration

blocking_assignment ::=
    reg_lvalue = [delay_or_event_control] expression

case_item ::=
    expression { , expression } : statement_or_null
    | **default** [:] statement_or_null

case_statement ::=
    case (expression) case_item { case_item } **endcase**
    | **casez** (expression) case_item { case_item } **endcase**
    | **casex** (expression) case_item { case_item } **endcase**

charge_strength ::=
    (**small**)
    | (**medium**)
    | (**large**)

cmos_switch_instance ::=
    [name_of_gate_instance] (output_terminal , input_terminal ,
    ncontrol_terminal , pcontrol_terminal)

cmos_switchtype ::=
    cmos | **rcmos**

combinational_body ::=
    table
        combinational_entry { combinational_entry }
    endtable

combinational_entry ::=
    level_input_list : output_symbol ;

comment ::=
    short_comment
    | long_comment

comment_text ::=
    { ANY_ASCII_CHARACTER }

concatenation ::=
    { expression { , expression } }

conditional_statement ::=
    if (expression) statement_or_null [**else** statement_or_null]

constant_expression ::=
    constant_primary
  | unary_operator constant_primary
  | constant_expression binary_operator constant_expression
  | constant_expression ? constant_expression : constant_expression
  | string

constant_mintypmax_expression ::=
    constant_expression
  | constant_expression : constant_expression : constant_expression

constant_primary ::=
    number
  | *parameter*_identifier
  | *constant*_concatenation
  | *constant*_multiple_concatenation

continuous_assign ::=
    assign [drive_strength] [delay3] list_of_net_assignments ;

controlled_timing_check_event ::=
    timing_check_event_control specify_terminal_descriptor
    [**&&&** timing_check_condition]

current_state ::=
    level_symbol

data_source_expression ::=
    expression

decimal_base ::=
    'd | **'D**

decimal_digit ::=
    0 | **1** | **2** | **3** | **4** | **5** | **6** | **7** | **8** | **9**

decimal_number ::=
    [sign] unsigned_number
  | [size] decimal_base unsigned_number

delay2 ::=
    # delay_value
  | # (delay_value [, delay_value])

delay3 ::=
    # delay_value
  | # (delay_value [, delay_value [, delay_value]])

delay_control ::=
    # delay_value
  | # (mintypmax_expression)

delay_or_event_control ::=
    delay_control

    | event_control
    | **repeat** (expression) event_control

delay_value ::=
    unsigned_number
    | parameter_identifier
    | constant_mintypmax_expression

description ::=
    module_declaration
    | udp_declaration

disable_statement ::=
    disable *task*_identifier ;
    | **disable** *block*_identifier ;

drive_strength ::=
    (strength0 , strength1)
    | (strength1 , strength0)
    | (strength0 , **highz1**)
    | (strength1 , **highz0**)
    | (**highz1** , strength0)
    | (**highz0** , strength1)

edge_control_specifier ::=
    edge [edge_descriptor [, edge_descriptor]]

edge_descriptor ::=
    01
    | **10**
    | **0x**
    | **x1**
    | **1x**
    | **x0**

edge_identifier ::=
    posedge | **negedge**

edge_indicator ::=
    (level_symbol level_symbol)
    | edge_symbol

edge_input_list ::=
    { level_symbol } edge_indicator { level_symbol }

edge_sensitive_path_declaration ::=
    parallel_edge_sensitive_path_description = path_delay_value
    | full_edge_sensitive_path_description = path_delay_value

edge_symbol ::=
    r | **R** | **f** | **F** | **p** | **P** | **n** | **N** | *****

enable_gate_instance ::=
    [name_of_gate_instance] (output_terminal , input_terminal ,
    enable_terminal)

enable_gate_type ::=
    bufif0 I **bufif1** I **notif0** I **notif1**

enable_terminal ::=
    *scalar*_expression

escaped_identifier ::=
    \ { ANY_ASCII_CHARACTER_EXCEPT_WHITE_SPACE } white_space

event_control ::=
    @ *event*_identifier
    I @ (event_expression)

event_declaration ::=
    event *event*_identifier { , *event*_identifier } ;

event_expression ::=
    expression
    I *event*_identifier
    I **posedge** expression
    I **negedge** expression
    I event_expression **or** event_expression

event_trigger ::=
    -> *event*_identifier ;

expression ::=
    primary
    I unary_operator primary
    I expression binary_operator expression
    I expression ? expression : expression
    I string

full_edge_sensitive_path_description ::=
    ([edge_identifier] list_of_path_inputs *> list_of_path_outputs
    [polarity_operator] : data_source_expression)

full_path_description ::=
    (list_of_path_inputs [polarity_operator] *> list_of_path_outputs)

function_call ::=
    *function*_identifier (expression { , expression })
    I name_of_system_function [(expression { , expression })]

function_declaration ::=
    function [range_or_type] *function*_identifier ;
        function_item_declaration { function_item_declaration }
        statement
    endfunction

function_item_declaration ::=
    block_item_declaration
    I   input_declaration

gate_instantiation ::=
        n_input_gatetype [drive_strength] [delay2] n_input_gate_instance
          { , n_input_gate_instance } ;
    | n_output_gatetype [drive_strength] [delay2] n_output_gate_instance
          { , n_output_gate_instance } ;
    | enable_gatetype [drive_strength] [delay3] enable_gate_instance
          { , enable_gate_instance } ;
    | mos_switchtype [delay3] mos_switch_instance
          { , mos_switch_instance } ;
    | pass_switchtype pass_switch_instance { , pass_switch_instance } ;
    | pass_en_switchtype [delay3] pass_en_switch_instance
          { , pass_en_switch_instance } ;
    | cmos_switchtype [delay3] cmos_switch_instance
          { , cmos_switch_instance } ;
    | **pullup** [pullup_strength] pull_gate_instance { , pull_gate_instance } ;
    | **pulldown** [pulldown_strength] pull_gate_instance
          { , pull_gate_instance } ;

hex_base ::=
    'h | **'H**

hex_digit ::=
      x | **X** | **z** | **Z**
    | **0** | **1** | **2** | **3** | **4** | **5** | **6** | **7** | **8** | **9**
    | **a** | **b** | **c** | **d** | **e** | **f** | **A** | **B** | **C** | **D** | **E** | **F**

hex_number ::=
    [size] hex_base hex_digit { _ | hex_digit }

identifier :=
    IDENTIFIER [{ . IDENTIFIER }]
    /* The period may not be followed or preceded by a space */

IDENTIFIER ::=
      simple_identifier
    | escaped_identifier

init_val ::=
    1'b0 | **1'b1** | **1'bx** | **1'bX** | **1'B0** | **1'B1** | **1'Bx** | **1'BX** | **1** | **0**

initial_construct ::=
    initial
    statement

inout_declaration ::=
    inout [range] list_of_port_identifiers ;

inout_terminal ::=
      *terminal*_identifier
    | *terminal*_identifier [constant_expression]

input_declaration ::=
    input [range] list_of_port_identifiers ;

input_identifier ::=
    *input_port*_identifier
    | *inout_port*_identifier

input_terminal ::=
    *scalar*_expression

integer_declaration ::=
    integer list_of_register_identifiers ;

level_input_list ::=
    level_symbol { level_symbol }

level_symbol ::=
    0 | 1 | x | X | ? | b | B

limit_value ::=
    constant_mintypmax_expression

list_of_module_connections ::=
    ordered_port_connection { , ordered_port_connection }
    | named_port_connection { , named_port_connection }

list_of_net_assignments ::=
    net_assignment { , net_assignment }

list_of_net_decl_assignments ::=
    net_decl_assignment { , net_decl_assignment }

list_of_net_identifiers ::=
    *net*_identifier { , *net*_identifier }

list_of_param_assignments ::=
    param_assignment { , param_assignment }

list_of_path_delay_expressions ::=
    *t*_path_delay_expression
    | *trise*_path_delay_expression , *tfall*_path_delay_expression
    | *trise*_path_delay_expression , *tfall*_path_delay_expression ,
        *tz*_path_delay_expression
    | *t01*_path_delay_expression , *t10*_path_delay_expression ,
        *t0z*_path_delay_expression , *tz1*_path_delay_expression ,
        *t1z*_path_delay_expression , *tz0*_path_delay_expression
    | *t01*_path_delay_expression , *t10*_path_delay_expression ,
        *t0z*_path_delay_expression , *tz1*_path_delay_expression ,
        *t1z*_path_delay_expression , *tz0*_path_delay_expression ,
        *t0x*_path_delay_expression , *tx1*_path_delay_expression ,
        *t1x*_path_delay_expression , *tx0*_path_delay_expression ,
        *txz*_path_delay_expression , *tzx*_path_delay_expression

list_of_path_inputs ::=
    specify_input_terminal_descriptor { , specify_input_terminal_descriptor }

list_of_path_outputs ::=
    specify_output_terminal_descriptor { , specify_output_terminal_descriptor }

list_of_port_identifiers ::=
    *port*_identifer { , *port*_identifier }

list_of_ports ::=
    (port { , port })

list_of_real_identifiers ::=
    *real*_identifier { , *real*_identifier }

list_of_register_identifiers ::=
    register_name { , register_name }

list_of_specparam_assignments ::=
    specparam_assignment { , specparam_assignment }

long_comment ::=
    /* comment_text */

loop_statement ::=
    forever statement
    | **repeat** (expression) statement
    | **while** (expression) statement
    | **for** (reg_assignment ; expression ; reg_assignment) statement

mintypmax_expression ::=
    expression
    | expression : expression : expression

module_declaration ::=
    module_keyword *module*_identifier [list_of_ports] ;
      { module_item }
    endmodule

module_instance ::=
    name_of_instance ([list_of_module_connections])

module_instantiation ::=
    *module*_identifier [parameter_value_assignment] module_instance
      { , module_instance } ;

module_item ::=
    module_item_declaration
    | parameter_override
    | continuous_assign
    | gate_instantiation
    | udp_instantiation
    | module_instantiation
    | specify_block
    | initial_construct
    | always_construct

module_item_declaration ::=
    parameter_declaration
    | input_declaration
    | output_declaration

| inout_declaration
| net_declaration
| reg_declaration
| integer_declaration
| real_declaration
| time_declaration
| realtime_declaration
| event_declaration
| task_declaration
| function_declaration

module_keyword ::=
  module | **macromodule**

mos_switch_instance ::=
  [name_of_gate_instance] (output_terminal , input_terminal ,
    enable_terminal)

mos_switchtype ::=
  nmos | **pmos** | **rnmos** | **rpmos**

multiple_concatenation ::=
  { expression { expression { , expression } } }

n_input_gate_instance ::=
  [name_of_gate_instance] (output_terminal , input_terminal
    { , input_terminal })

n_input_gatetype ::=
  and | **nand** | **or** | **nor** | **xor** | **xnor**

n_output_gate_instance ::=
  [name_of_gate_instance] (output_terminal { , output_terminal } ,
    input_terminal)

n_output_gatetype ::=
  buf | **not**

name_of_gate_instance ::=
  *gate_instance_*identifier [range]

name_of_instance ::=
  *module_instance_*identifier [range]

name_of_system_function ::=
  $identifier

name_of_udp_instance ::=
  *udp_instance_*identifier [range]

named_port_connection ::=
  . *port_*identifier ([expression])

ncontrol_terminal ::=
  *scalar_*expression

net_assignment ::=
    net_lvalue = expression

net_decl_assignment ::=
    *net*_identifier = expression

net_declaration ::=
      net_type [**vectored** | **scalared**] [range] [delay3] list_of_net_identifiers **;**
    | **trireg** [**vectored** | **scalared**] [charge_strength] [range] [delay3]
      list_of_net_identifiers **;**
    | net_type [**vectored** | **scalared**] [drive_strength] [range] [delay3]
      list_of_net_decl_assignments **;**

net_lvalue ::=
    *net*_identifier
    | *net*_identifier [expression]
    | *net*_identifier [*msb*_constant_expression **:** *lsb*_constant_expression]
    | *net*_concatenation

net_type ::=
    wire | **tri** | **tri1** | **supply0** | **wand** | **triand** | **tri0** | **supply1** | **wor** | **trior**

next_state ::=
    output_symbol | **-**

non_blocking_assignment ::=
    reg_lvalue <= [delay_or_event_control] expression

notify_register ::=
    *register*_identifier

number ::=
    decimal_number
    | octal_number
    | binary_number
    | hex_number
    | real_number

octal_base ::=
    'o | **'O**

octal_digit ::=
    x | **X** | **z** | **Z** | **0** | **1** | **2** | **3** | **4** | **5** | **6** | **7**

octal_number ::=
    [size] octal_base octal_digit { **_** | octal_digit }

ordered_port_connection ::=
    [expression]

output_declaration ::=
    output [range] list_of_port_identifiers **;**

output_identifier ::=
    *output_port*_identifier
    | *inout_port*_identifier

output_symbol ::=
    0 | **1** | **x** | **X**

output_terminal ::=
    *terminal_*identifier
    | *terminal_*identifier [constant_expression]

par_block ::=
    fork
      [**:** *block_*identifier
        { block_item_declaration }]
      { statement }
    join

parallel_edge_sensitive_path_description ::=
    ([edge_identifier] specify_input_terminal_descriptor **=>**
      specify_output_terminal_descriptor [polarity_operator] **:**
      data_source_expression **)**

parallel_path_description ::=
    (specify_input_terminal_descriptor [polarity_operator] **=>**
      specify_output_terminal_descriptor **)**

param_assignment ::=
    *parameter_*identifier = constant_expression

parameter_declaration ::=
    parameter list_of_param_assignments **;**

parameter_override ::=
    defparam list_of_param_assignments **;**

parameter_value_assignment ::=
    # (expression { **,** expression })

pass_en_switchtype ::=
    tranif0 | **tranif1** | **rtranif1** | **rtranif0**

pass_en_switch_instance ::=
    [name_of_gate_instance] (inout_terminal , inout_terminal ,
      enable_terminal)

pass_switch_instance ::=
    [name_of_gate_instance] (inout_terminal , inout_terminal)

pass_switchtype ::=
    tran | **rtran**

path_declaration ::=
    simple_path_declaration **;**
    | edge_sensitive_path_declaration **;**
    | state_dependent_path_declaration **;**

path_delay_expression ::=
    constant_mintypmax_expression

path_delay_value ::=
  list_of_path_delay_expressions
  | (list_of_path_delay_expressions)

pcontrol_terminal ::=
  *scalar*_expression

polarity_operator ::=
  + | -

port ::=
  [port_expression]
  | . *port*_identifier ([port_expression])

port_expression ::=
  port_reference
  | { port_reference { , port_reference } }

port_reference ::=
  *port*_identifier
  | *port*_identifier [constant_expression]
  | *port*_identifier [*msb*_constant_expression : *lsb*_constant_expression]

primary ::=
  number
  | identifier
  | identifier [expression]
  | identifier [*msb*_constant_expression : *lsb*_constant_expression]
  | concatenation
  | multiple_concatenation
  | function_call
  | (mintypmax_expression)

procedural_continuous_assignment ::=
  assign reg_assignment ;
  | **deassign** reg_lvalue ;
  | **force** reg_assignment ;
  | **force** net_assignment ;
  | **release** reg_lvalue ;
  | **release** net_lvalue ;

procedural_timing_control_statement ::=
  delay_or_event_control statement_or_null

pull_gate_instance ::=
  [name_of_gate_instance] (output_terminal)

pulldown_strength ::=
  (strength0 , strength1)
  | (strength1 , strength0)
  | (strength0)

pullup_strength ::=
  (strength0 , strength1)

    | (strength1 , strength0)
    | (strength1)

pulse_control_specparam ::=
    PATHPULSE$ = (*reject*_limit_value [, *error*_limit_value]) **;**
    | **PATHPULSE$**specify_input_terminal_descriptor /**no space; continue**/
    $specify_output_terminal_descriptor = (*reject*_limit_value
    [, *error*_limit_value]) **;**[1]

range ::=
    [*msb*_constant_expression : *lsb*_constant_expression]

range_or_type ::=
    range | **integer** | **real** | **realtime** | **time**

real_declaration ::=
    real list_of_real_identifiers **;**

real_number ::=
    [sign] unsigned_number **.** unsigned_number
    | [sign] unsigned_number [**.** unsigned_number] **e** [sign]
       unsigned_number
    | [sign] unsigned_number [**.** unsigned_number] **E** [sign]
       unsigned_number

realtime_declaration ::=
    realtime list_of_real_identifiers **;**

reg_assignment ::=
    reg_lvalue = expression

reg_declaration ::=
    reg [range] list_of_register_identifiers **;**

reg_lvalue ::=
    *reg*_identifier
    | *reg*_identifier [expression]
    | *reg*_identifier [*msb*_constant_expression : *lsb*_constant_expression]
    | *reg*_concatenation

register_name ::=
    *register*_identifier
    | *memory*_identifier [*upper_limit*_constant_expression :
       *lower_limit*_constant_expression]

scalar_constant ::=
    1'b0 | **1'b1** | **1'B0** | **1'B1** | **'b0** | **'b1** | **'B0** | **'B1** | **1** | **0**

scalar_timing_check_condition ::=
    expression
    | ~ expression
    | expression == scalar_constant

---

1. For example, **PATHPULSECLKQ** = (5, 3);

    | expression === scalar_constant
    | expression != scalar_constant
    | expression !== scalar_constant

seq_block ::=
    begin
      [: *block*_identifier
        { block_item_declaration }]
      { statement }
    end

seq_input_list ::=
    level_input_list | edge_input_list

sequential_body ::=
    [udp_initial_statement]
    table
      sequential_entry
      { sequential_entry }
    endtable

sequential_entry ::=
    seq_input_list : current_state : next_state ;

short_comment ::=
    // comment_text \n

sign ::=
    + | -

simple_identifier ::=
    [a-zA-Z][a-zA-Z_$0-9]

simple_path_declaration ::=
      parallel_path_description = path_delay_value
    | full_path_description = path_delay_value

size ::=
    unsigned_number

source_text ::=
    { description }

specify_block ::=
    specify
      { specify_item }
    endspecify

specify_input_terminal_descriptor ::=
      input_identifier
    | input_identifier [constant_expression]
    | input_identifier [*msb*_constant_expression : *lsb*_constant_expression]

specify_item ::=
    specparam_declaration

    | path_declaration
    | system_timing_check

specify_output_terminal_descriptor ::=
    output_identifier
    | output_identifier [constant_expression]
    | output_identifier [*msb*_constant_expression : *lsb*_constant_expression]

specify_terminal_descriptor ::=
    specify_input_terminal_descriptor
    | specify_output_terminal_descriptor

specparam_assignment ::=
    *specparam*_identifier = constant_expression
    | pulse_control_specparam

specparam_declaration ::=
    specparam list_of_specparam_assignments ;

state_dependent_path_declaration ::=
    if (*conditional*_expression) simple_path_declaration
    | **if** (*conditional*_expression) edge_sensitive_path_declaration
    | **ifnone** simple_path_declaration

statement ::=
    blocking_assignment ;
    | non_blocking_assignment ;
    | procedural_continuous_assignment ;
    | procedural_timing_control_statement
    | conditional_statement
    | case_statement
    | loop_statement
    | wait_statement
    | disable_statement
    | event_trigger
    | seq_block
    | par_block
    | task_enable
    | system_task_enable

statement_or_null ::=
    statement | ;

strength0 ::=
    supply0 | **strong0** | **pull0** | **weak0**

strength1 ::=
    supply1 | **strong1** | **pull1** | **weak1**

string ::=
    " { ANY_ASCII_CHARACTERS_EXCEPT_NEWLINE } "

system_task_enable ::=
    system_task_name [(expression { , expression })] ;

system_task_name ::=
    $identifier
    /* The $ cannot be followed by a space */

system_timing_check ::=
      $setup (timing_check_event , timing_check_event , timing_check_limit
        [, notify_register]) ;
    | **$hold** (timing_check_event , timing_check_event , timing_check_limit
        [, notify_register]) ;
    | **$period** (controlled_timing_check_event , timing_check_limit
        [, notify_register]) ;
    | **$width** (controlled_timing_check_event , timing_check_limit ,
        constant_expression [, notify_register]) ;
    | **$skew** (timing_check_event , timing_check_event , timing_check_limit
        [, notify_register]) ;
    | **$recovery** (controlled_timing_check_event , timing_check_event ,
        timing_check_limit [, notify_tegister]) ;
    | **$setuphold** (timing_check_event , timing_check_event ,
        timing_check_limit , timing_check_limit [, notify_register]) ;

task_declaration ::=
    task *task*_identifier ;
    { task_item_declaration }
    statement_or_null
    endtask

task_enable ::=
    *task*_identifier [(expression { , expression })] ;

task_item_declaration ::=
    block_item_declaration
    | input_declaration
    | output_declaration
    | inout_declaration

time_declaration ::=
    time list_of_register_identifiers ;

timing_check_condition ::=
    scalar_timing_check_condition
    | (scalar_timing_check_condition)

timing_check_event ::=
    [timing_check_event_control] specify_terminal_descriptor
    [&&& timing_check_condition]

timing_check_event_control ::=
    posedge
    | **negedge**
    | edge_control_specifier

timing_check_limit ::=
    expression

udp_body ::=
    combinational_body
  | sequential_body

udp_declaration ::=
    primitive *udp*_identifier (udp_port_list) ;
    udp_port_declaration
    { udp_port_declaration }
    udp_body
    endprimitive

udp_initial_statement ::=
    initial *udp_output_port*_identifier = init_val ;

udp_instance ::=
    [name_of_udp_instance] (output_port_connection , input_port_connection
    { , input_port_connection })

udp_instantiation ::=
    *udp*_identifier [drive_strength] [delay2] udp_instance { , udp_instance } ;

udp_port_declaration ::=
    output_declaration
  | input_declaration
  | reg_declaration

udp_port_list ::=
    *output_port*_identifier , *input_port*_identifier { , *input_port*_identifier }

unary_operator ::=
    + | - | ! | ~ | & | ~& | | | ~| | ^ | ~^ | ^~

unsigned_number ::=
    decimal_digit { _ | decimal_digit }

wait_statement ::=
    wait (expression) statement_or_null

white_space ::=
    space | tab | newline

❏

BIBLIOGRAPHY

1. Arnold M., *Verilog Digital Computer Design: Algorithms to Hardware*, Prentice Hall, NJ, 1998.

2. Bhasker J., *Verilog HDL Synthesis: A Practical Primer*, Star Galaxy Publishing, PA, 1998, ISBN 0-9650391-5-3.

3. Lee J., *Verilog Quickstart*, Kluwer Academic, MA, 1997.

4. Palnitkar S., *Verilog HDL: A Guide to Digital Design and Synthesis*, Prentice Hall, NJ, 1996, ISBN 0-13-451675-3.

5. Sagdeo V., *Complete Verilog Book*, Kluwer Academic, MA, 1998.

6. Smith D., *HDL Chip Design*, Doone Publications, 1996.

7. Sternheim E., R. Singh and Y. Trivedi, *Digital Design and Synthesis with Verilog HDL*, Automata Publishing Company, CA, 1993.

8. Thomas D. and P. Moorby, *The Verilog Hardware Description Language*, Kluwer Academic, MA, 1991, ISBN 0-7923-9126-8.

9. *IEEE Standard Hardware Description Language Based on the Verilog Hardware Description Language*, IEEE Std 1364-1995, IEEE, 1995.

10. Open Verilog International, *OVI Standard Delay File (SDF) Format Manual*.

❏

INDEX

❑

Order Form

☆ **Fax orders**: (610) 391-7296

☆ **Telephone orders**: Call toll free (888) 727-7296

☆ **On-line orders**: SGalaxyPub@aol.com

☆ **Web site orders**: http://users.aol.com/SGalaxyPub

☆ **Postal orders**: Star Galaxy Publishing, Suite 401, 1058 Treeline Drive, Allentown, PA 18103.

Yes!!!! Please send me:

__ copies of *A VHDL Synthesis Primer, Second Edition* by J. Bhasker, ISBN 0-9650391-9-6, $59.95*

__ copies of *A Verilog HDL Primer, Second Edition* by J. Bhasker, ISBN 0-9650391-7-X, $64.95*

__ copies of *Verilog HDL Synthesis, A Practical Primer* by J. Bhasker, ISBN 0-9650391-5-3, $49.95*
* For orders of 3 or more, see http://users.aol.com/SGalaxyPub for discount schedule

I understand that I may return the books for a full refund - for any reason, no questions asked.

Name: _____

Address: _____

City: _____ State: _____ Zip: _____-_____

Telephone: (____) _____ Email: _____

Sales tax:
Please add 6% for books shipped to Pennsylvania addresses.

Shipping:
○ Delivery less than 1 week : $5.00 for first book, $0.50 for each additional book via UPS Ground or equivalent.
○ Delivery 1 to 2 weeks : $3.20 per book via USPS Priority Mail
○ International addresses: $7.00 to $15.00 per book via air mail depending on country

Payment:
❏ Cheque (payable to *Star Galaxy Publishing*)
❏ Credit card: ○ VISA ○ MasterCard ○ AMEX
  ❏ Card number: _____
  ❏ Name on card:_____Exp. date: _____/_____
  ❏ Signature: _____

Call *toll free* and order now!

Order Form

☆ **Fax orders**: (610) 391-7296

☆ **Telephone orders**: Call toll free (888) 727-7296

☆ **On-line orders**: SGalaxyPub@aol.com

☆ **Web site orders**: http://users.aol.com/SGalaxyPub

☆ **Postal orders**: Star Galaxy Publishing, Suite 401, 1058 Treeline Drive, Allentown, PA 18103.

Yes!!!! Please send me:

__ copies of *A VHDL Synthesis Primer, Second Edition* by J. Bhasker, ISBN 0-9650391-9-6, $59.95*

__ copies of *A Verilog HDL Primer, Second Edition* by J. Bhasker, ISBN 0-9650391-7-X, $64.95*

__ copies of *Verilog HDL Synthesis, A Practical Primer* by J. Bhasker, ISBN 0-9650391-5-3, $49.95*
* For orders of 3 or more, see http://users.aol.com/SGalaxyPub for discount schedule

I understand that I may return the books for a full refund - for any reason, no questions asked.

Name: _____

Address: _____

City: _____ State: _____ Zip: _____-_____

Telephone: (____) _____ Email: _____

Sales tax:
Please add 6% for books shipped to Pennsylvania addresses.

Shipping:
○ Delivery less than 1 week : $5.00 for first book, $0.50 for each additional book via UPS Ground or equivalent.
○ Delivery 1 to 2 weeks : $3.20 per book via USPS Priority Mail
○ International addresses: $7.00 to $15.00 per book via air mail depending on country

Payment:
❏ Cheque (payable to *Star Galaxy Publishing*)
❏ Credit card: ○ VISA ○ MasterCard ○ AMEX
   ❏ Card number: _____
   ❏ Name on card:_____Exp. date: _____/_____
   ❏ Signature: _____

Call *toll free* and order now!